God's Amazing Grace

My Story

Dr. Thelma Nicholls

TEACH Services, Inc.
P U B L I S H I N G
www.TEACHServices.com • (800) 367-1844

Copyright © 2022 Dr. Thelma Nicholls

Copyright © 2022 TEACH Services, Inc.

ISBN-13: 978-1-4796-0967-3 (Paperback)

ISBN-13: 978-1-4796-0968-0 (ePub)

Library of Congress Control Number: 2021922991

All scripture quotations, unless otherwise indicated, are taken from the New King James Version®. Copyright © 1982 by Thomas Nelson. Used by permission. All rights reserved.

Scripture quotations marked (NIV) are taken from the Holy Bible, New International Version®, NIV®. Copyright © 1973, 1978, 1984, 2011 by Biblica, Inc.™ Used by permission of Zondervan. All rights reserved worldwide. www.zondervan.com. The "NIV" and "New International Version" are trademarks registered in the United States Patent and Trademark Office by Biblica, Inc.™

The website references in this book have been shortened using a URL shortener and redirect service called 1ref.us, which TEACH Services manages. If you find that a reference no longer works, please contact us and let us know which one is not working so that we can correct it. Any personal website addresses that the author included are managed by the author. TEACH Services is not responsible for the accuracy or permanency of any links.

Some of the names in this book have been changed to protect the identity and privacy of the individuals.

TEACH Services, Inc.
P U B L I S H I N G
www.TEACHServices.com ● (800) 367-1844

Dedication

First and foremost, I give God the glory for the work He has done in me. Also, the work He has allowed me to do. This book is also dedicated to my dear husband, Robert, who has been my support, standing by me through the ups and downs of this journey. When I felt like giving up, he constantly offered me the love and encouragement to continue. Not only did he help my spiritual life grow to maturity but also helped me become the best that I could be.

Table of Contents

Preface...7

List of Abbreviations...9

Chapter 1...11

Chapter 2...18

Chapter 3...22

Chapter 4...28

Chapter 5...33

Chapter 6...36

Chapter 7...41

Chapter 8...48

Chapter 9...51

Chapter 10...55

Chapter 11...60

Chapter 12...66

Chapter 13...70

Chapter 14...73

Chapter 15...78

Chapter 16...81

Chapter 17...84

Chapter 18...88

Chapter 19...93

Glossary...97

Bibliography...103

Index 104

Preface

I have spent most of my life seeking to improve myself through either education or training. Although I did work with another author as a typist in one of my many careers, I never imagined formally writing down my own story. As a part of my constant drive, though, I did eventually end up studying for my doctoral degree. The capstone project for any graduate degree requires a publication of some sort, and that is when I looked into options for publishing my work.

TEACH Services, Inc. helped me through the process, which included creating a brief biography that tells about me, the author of my dissertation. As I thought about the most important parts of my life to include in this, it re-affirmed what I knew in my heart all along: that I had a story to tell that may inspire others to persevere. I've always kept a journal for this reason because I knew someday, somehow, I needed to let others know how God maneuvered my journey in life.

It was then that I decided to embark on a new path of learning—that all-important path of self-discovery. It is my hope in writing this that you will understand that whatever you are going through, God is there for you—listening and gently guiding your life in the direction that He knows is best for you and providing you with opportunities to be a witness for His Kingdom.

List of Abbreviations

CT scan	:	Computerized Tomography scan
ICU	:	Intensive Care Unit
JAMINTEL	:	Jamaica International Telecommunications Limited
JLP	:	Jamaica Labor Party
NCO	:	Non-Commissioned Officer
MED BOARD	:	Medical Evaluation Board
PICU	:	Pediatric Intensive Care Unit
PNP	:	People's National Party
PTSD	:	Post-Traumatic Stress Disorder
ROSCA	:	Rotating Savings and Credit Associations
ROTC	:	Reserve Officers' Training Corps
SDA	:	Seventh-day Adventist

Chapter 1

Jamaica Map

When many people think of Jamaica, they think of the tropical beach resorts surrounded by high walls and fun in the sun. In Kingston where I was born, a regular city exists with rich and poor neighborhoods. I was born June 26, 1956, and my first home was not behind the walls of a resort but behind the walls of a tenement yard.

The tenement yard wall enclosed a few one- and two-story homes that were small. As with most third-world countries, we didn't have the luxury of indoor plumbing and, in some cases, indoor kitchens. Instead, there were two or three kitchens that were shared by the occupants. The two bathrooms outside were also shared by the tenants of the yard. Please understand this was one area where I lived. As I grew up, I lived in other areas of Jamaica where I had my own bathroom and own kitchen.

Duke Street in Kingston

Violence was a part of everyday life on the island. I witnessed it inside and outside the home. You see, in Jamaica, elections are run quite differently from those in America. Jamaica was still under colonial control when the Great Depression hit in the 1930s. There had long been unemployment problems and poor working conditions prior to this time, but just as the early 1900s caused unions in America to rise, the worsening conditions of the Great Depression caused two cousins, William Alexander Bustamante and Norman W. Manley, to create the earliest labor unions in Jamaica. Because of the civil unrest, police and eventually the unions fought against each other, which sometimes culminated in riots. By 1944, the British recognized the problems with the "British West Indies" (of which Jamaica was a part at that time) and began transitioning the islands toward independence by instituting limited self-government.

At that time, the two major unions also transitioned into the two major political parties: the Jamaica Labor Party (JLP), led by Bustamante and the People's National Party (PNP), led by Manley. With the British stepping away from the fight, the supporters of the two unions-turned-political parties began to use violence against the opposing party. This is a tradition that has continued to develop throughout the decades (Williams, 2011).

Needless to say, growing up in a Jamaican tenement yard during a few elections was a scary time for me. I remember trying to stay inside as much as possible because outside, men and boys would be carrying large guns—rifles and even machine guns—and jumping from roof to roof in displays of power.

The best part of growing up in those areas was that it was like growing up in an area surrounded by extended family. Being an only child with the lack of support, guidance, or love in my own home, sometimes I took refuge at an early age in visiting a neighbor's home to look at his books. I loved to read. It took my mind to places of peace and quietness. Places where I would imagine a good life—something different from what I had. "Maas" Vin made kitchen graters to grate coconut and other foods. He managed to accumulate several books, and I took pleasure in looking at them even before I could understand everything I was reading. One book had a picture in it that fascinated me. On one side of the picture was a small village with a large, wide road running through the center of the picture. There were trees all around, and in the sky, stars were falling (Smith, *Daniel and the Revelation*, p. 422). I often wondered what it would be like to be there in the middle of such a beautiful display.

Another fond memory I have is when my uncles and other men would go fishing or take me fishing, and we would get together on the beach and cook everything that was caught. This time at the beach occupied my mind and kept me away from the sad home life in which I was raised. It also was some of the best-tasting food. Because this is one of the few good memories I had as a child, when I became an Adventist, it was extremely difficult for me to give up shellfish. **Apart from the shellfish, there were many other good memories. I enjoyed the association with my uncles.** As Christians, we are quick to dish out the dos and do nots before we apply God's instructions and His grace. Fruit trees bear specific fruits because it is their nature to do so. We do not do works to become Christians. We do them because we are Christians!

I believe the Holy Spirit also allowed me to escape the hurt and pain I experienced during my dreams at night. In one particular repetitive dream, I would be on the one side of a dry, barren land with a crystal clear stream down the middle, and on the other side was a beautiful, luscious, green meadow. I would yearn to get across but would always hear a voice telling me it would be like looking for a needle in a haystack. When I awoke, I would be so disappointed. The saddest part was that even as I dreamed, I could not find a way across the water.

As I grew, I made it to sixth form (eleventh grade) by the time I was sixteen: to continue beyond that depended entirely on how well I did on the equivalent of a college entrance exam. I knew my parents did not have much money. In fact, I do not remember them doing much work at all while I was growing up until my father went to work at the Jamaica International Telecommunications Limited (JAMINTEL) as a security guard in the 1970s.

Even as a teen, I had a strong desire to make myself better by continuing my education. I studied hard, but sadly my grade on the exam only allowed for half a scholarship, and my parents refused to pay anything for further education.

It was around this time that my father began abusing me sexually. My mother, who had grown used to his extramarital affairs and half-siblings wandering in and out of our house to see him, did nothing to stop this abuse. If I tried to fight back, I was physically abused as well. The one-room home became claustrophobic. I never knew when he would appear, and there was nowhere to hide inside it.

Our house was next door to JAMINTEL, and one day, I went to take my father his lunch. A tall, South African man with tinted green glasses by the name of Mr. Fowler was with him and asked, "Is this her?"

> *I still needed to escape my home life as the abuse intensified.*

My father replied, "Yes." My father had apparently arranged to sell me to him. I went to my mother and told her. It was one of the few times I saw her stand up to my father. I now see in this moment of bravery on my mother's part that the hand of God was working to protect me and guide me into His arms. Had I been sold at that time; I would never have had the opportunities to attend church and learn about Him. Looking back, this was probably the first miracle God performed in my life, even though I did not understand everything that was happening then.

I still needed to escape my home life as the abuse intensified. If you are reading this and you are a teacher or student, the following might sound strange, but reflect on the title of my book. I completed the sixth form, and with nowhere to go and no future to look forward to, I came up with a plan. Back then, in Jamaica, with a half scholarship, the government would pay a portion of your continued schooling, and your parents would pay the difference. Otherwise, you had to quit school. I never reported my parents were not interested in paying my portion, so I ended up with my school uniform, books, and supplies for the beginning of the school term. On the first day of school, I showed up to class in the school for which I had the half scholarship. There was no roll call, so there was no problem with me being there. I showed up to class each day for quite a while until someone realized I did not belong there. That discovery did not stop me. I just went to another classroom. I kept switching classrooms as soon as I was found out until I could not do it anymore. I finally ended up in the headmaster's office, where it was discovered my school fee was not paid in full, so I had to leave the school.

My life was at a standstill again, but my mind was still searching for a way to get out of the life and the environment in which I found myself. I learned about a government program linked to a certain political party that would allow me to attend secretarial school. Of course, I jumped at the opportunity and did very well. It was not too long into my studies that my father said I had to stop and find a job because we needed more money for the household. I found a job at a haberdashery store and worked seven days per week. I would bring home the money and give it to my father. I would only get back money for lunch sometimes. There is one time I will never forget when the store had gotten a new style of shoes. That Friday, when I got paid, I bought a pair of them before taking home the money. My father was so angry that if I had not left the house, there is no telling what would have happened.

Salvation Army Church, Kingston, Jamaica

I eventually lost that job because of union involvement. It was then my father called a friend who owned a nightclub and got me another job working there as a waitress. I would serve drinks until the early hours of the morning and then collapse from exhaustion in a back room. The owner would lock me in the room for my protection until she was ready to take me home. I think back now and know that despite the situation, God was guiding and protecting me from what could have been a more disastrous environment.

The owner of the nightclub eventually told my father the nightclub was not a place for me. She said she would not have her daughter working at a place like that, so she refused to take me back there to work. With no future plans and no guidance, I kept asking myself if my life was just going to end up like everyone else around me. I was filled with hate for my father. It was around that time I was exposed to the Salvation Army through a cousin of mine.

Most people see the Salvation Army bell ringers around Christmas and do not realize the Salvation Army is a church. It is a Christian denomination where the Bible is a major authority.

The Salvation Army Church was good at appealing to young people, especially to those of us in the poorer areas. They would have open-air meetings every Thursday night, and young and old would flock around to enjoy the music and preaching. I started attending, and on one occasion when they had an altar call, I went up and accepted Jesus as my Savior. I began attending church and was exposed to a different life.

All the while, I kept hidden the dirty secret that I was being abused by my father. Let me be clear at this point: He attempted to forcefully have sex with me, hitting me, touching my breast, and making other advances but never successfully completing his attempts. God always gave me the strength to get away by fighting him off, even though I endured a slap or a scar or some kind of physical abuse. I do not think I would have been able to live if he was able to actually have sex with me. Looking back on the person I was at that time, I think I would have taken his life then mine afterward.

While in the Salvation Army, I was adopted by Daniel, who was a very kind, father-like figure. He saw something in me and encouraged me to play the alto horn for Salvation Army functions. I wore my uniform with such pride every Sunday morning and Thursday evening. We had timbrel competitions, and I was so happy that others saw something in me. I fit in with everyone else, and the militaristic organization appealed to me in a time when the outside world was mostly chaos. Then, I was given the opportunity to preach my first sermon by Major Mason. It was on the Lord's Prayer. Imagine that? This girl, who was from "the other side of the tracks," as they would say, standing at the pulpit preaching. The time spent in the band gave me peace that I did not have at home, as well as a means of escaping the abuse.

Although I was attending church, a deep hatred burned inside of me. This hatred was sometimes all that kept me going from one day to the next, instead of the Joy of the Lord that now gives me strength. The anger inside me also fueled my strength to fight against my father. Throughout my childhood, I watched him abuse my mother and everyone around him, but as I grew older, I began fighting back harder each year. By fighting, I was only subject to physical abuse, which was easier for me to deal with emotionally.

At this time, while I was attending the Salvation Army Church, I developed a friendship with a guy who was attractive and kind to me. I had never had a relationship with another boy my age and only saw in this guy the good traits that I did not see in anyone else. He was from the "good" side of town, and it impressed me that he would pay attention to someone from my neighborhood. They all went to high school even without scholarships and had parents who had respectable jobs and went to church. None of them smoked or cussed.

His family was educated, and they easily funded his last years of high school. When we met, he was getting ready to graduate and had plans to attend the University of the West Indies. His parents and sisters disapproved of the relationship we had because they felt their son was better than me. That did not stop me from naïvely believing we would be great together. I used to go over to his house, and we would hang out and talk all the time. On one of those occasions, no one was at home and what was supposed to have been an innocent visit turned into my giving birth to my first child exactly one month after my twentieth birthday.

Chapter 2

In 1976, I began gaining weight. Daniel, in his usual jest, kept telling me to stop eating or I would not fit into my uniform any longer. I was pregnant!

Instead of reacting with joy to support my pregnancy, my family reacted to the news with anger. My father was irate. His reaction gave me no doubt that he had wanted to take my virginity and had been trying to prepare me so he could do just that. Since my parents had lived together out of wedlock my entire life and neither were religious, they did not talk about marriage or even consider anything like that.

Ben's parents were equally upset. He was still in school, pursuing his education. I did not have a job nor anything else to offer him. They could not believe their son would get someone "below their standard" pregnant. Although they split the blame equally between Ben and me, the maliciousness toward me was exceptionally painful. One of his sisters even told me she hoped that giving birth to the baby would kill me. Only one of his sisters spoke kindly with me and attempted to develop a relationship with me, and we remain friends.

Ben drank, and our relationship became just as abusive as the relationship I witnessed between my parents. There was no talk of marriage. From my parents' example, I did not think anything was wrong with that. I did hope he would move out of his parents' home and build a family with me. I was slightly scared because, in Jamaica, single mothers are put out of the church and out of their own parents' home. With Ben unwilling to step forward and create a home for us, I was uncertain where I could turn.

Sure enough, my father told me to leave the house. I had nowhere to go but on the street. A brother/sister family from the Salvation Army opened their home to me at first, but Ben kept visiting while they were not at home. I truly thought we would end up together eventually, and so I did nothing to prevent him from visiting. On one of those visits, he arrived drunk. I don't recall what prompted the reaction, but he began punching me. He left, but the evidence of his visit was all over my face in black and blue.

The family was shocked. They told me they were sorry, but I had to leave because they could not tolerate that kind of behavior in their home. They further explained that people in their neighborhood and in the church did not behave like that. It was raining that night, and I knew it hurt them to have me go, but I understood. None of us knew that night would become my first witness to a miracle.

Although the Lord closed that door, He was still watching out for me. I called a friend, whose name was Merthie, and told her I had nowhere to go. She told me I could come and stay with her until I found another place. However, she said she was not at home right then, but by the time I got there, she would not be long getting home. I packed my things quickly and boarded the bus in the rain to get to her home. As the bus traveled through an area where there was no rain, I watched the sun set through the bus window. I tried not to think about the physical pain from my swollen face and the emotional pain from being kicked out of yet another house.

Memories of my father sprang into my head, and I huddled outside with my belongings, waiting for the worst.

When I got to Merthie's house on the other side of town, it was raining again. I got off the bus and walked to her house. I was wet and tired, but she had not yet returned home from her work. The door was locked, so I checked under the mat, hoping to find a key. There was none. By that time, exhaustion had taken over, and I broke down in tears when I realized there was no way out of the rain since it was blowing onto the porch where I was standing.

With nothing else to do, I set my bag on the porch and sat down, shivering. I cried out to God, "Please, God, please help me. Please open the door for me. Please, let Merthie come and open the door for me." As tears and rain mixed together on my face, my prayer rose to the Lord, and the door slowly began to open.

My first thought was not that God had performed a miracle and opened the door but rather that someone else had opened the door and was waiting inside for me. So, I was ready to run for my life. Memories of my father sprang into my head, and I huddled outside with my belongings, waiting for the worst. When no one came out to grab me, I slowly gained enough courage to go inside. With a timid shove of the door, I could see the room was small, and no one was in it. I quickly peered behind the door where someone might be hiding, but no one was there either. I then cautiously went and looked under the bed, which was the last place anyone could have possibly hidden in the room.

After my inspection showed that there was not another person in the home with me, I quickly shut and locked the door. I certainly did not want someone wandering past and seeing me alone in there.

When Merthie arrived, she wondered how I had managed to enter her home. I asked her if maybe she had forgotten to lock the door, but Merthie insisted she had. Since I had tried to open the door myself, I knew this was true. If an earthquake had opened the door, I would have felt it. If the door was locked, but somehow the latch missed the striker, again, when I tried to open the door, it would have opened for me right away. Merthie and I puzzled over the situation for most of the evening. For some reason, I did not make the connection that the Lord was trying to get my attention. Now I realize, He was letting me know that He would take care of me if only I would put my trust in Him.

Merthie was kind to open her home to me on short notice, but her home was only one room, and we had to share one bed. With my growing stomach, things became uncomfortable for both of us. I didn't have a job at that point, so I tried to make the best I could of the situation. I was troubled that Merthie had to be inconvenienced, so I shared my discomfort with my mother. My mother offered to cash in her "partner" so I could have enough money to rent my own house in the same tenement yard as her.

Like many countries, Jamaica has banks, building and loans, and credit unions. Unique to Jamaica are private collectives known as rotating savings and credit associations (ROSCAs or "partners"). A group of people (usually women) appoint one trustworthy person to be the banker. The banker collects a regular amount from each person in the group every week. Each month, one draw is released to one of the members in an order determined by the banker. In return, the banker also gets a share of the money. If someone needs a loan, they can ask for a loan against their next draw. The banker is responsible for determining whether a person asking for money can receive the loan or not.

The Jamaicans prefer this system to banks because the people involved are forced to save. With banks and building and loan businesses, saving is not obligatory. Although credit unions sometimes allow members of the credit union to set aside a certain amount each paycheck, users can also withdraw from their savings whenever they wish. The partner system prevents people from withdrawing money regularly and allows them to save for specific big-ticket items.

My mother was a member of one of these collectives, and I assume this is how my father and she were able to save enough money to buy a store around this point in their lives. This time, when my mother received the draw from the partner, she gave the money to me so I could rent a room in their tenement yard.

The $17 for rent, $3 for water, and $5 for electricity were covered by my mother's generosity, but I could not afford any furniture. There was a lady downstairs who had her own business and was very "high color," even though she was living in the tenement yard. Her home had four or five rooms, and she even had a television that caused many of us to flock outside her door and peer in at it when our favorite shows, such as *Bonanza*, were playing. Since she was a dressmaker by trade, when she saw that I had no bed where I could comfortably sleep, she donated two bags of cloth scraps to me so I could use them as a bed. My mother had to wait another month to get another draw, but as soon as she did, we purchased a bed.

My first son was born in the hospital in Kingston on July 26, 1976. Exactly one month after my twentieth birthday, I simply got in the taxi, rode to the hospital, and the government paid for it. Giving birth for the first time and being faced with the new situation of raising a child were both daunting tasks, but I continued to look at each new thing as an opportunity to learn.

Chapter 3

After I had the baby, I was able to get a job working for the Salvation Army switchboard. That helped me pay for food, rent, and other necessities, but money was tight. Ben came to visit sometimes, and on the weekends, I would take my son to see his parents. They refused to let me near the house, so I would wait outside the fence for him to finish seeing them and come out to me. He was their first grandchild, so they eventually came to love him.

I did occasionally get a kind of child support, but Ben's mother thought she knew better than me about what was best for my child. In some ways, this was just another way of controlling how much money her son would give me for support.

I would not have any of her interference. I knew what my child needed and demanded to get what was his to spend how I saw fit to spend it on him. This caused friction and eventually ended up in stopping Ben's support of our child. As parents, we must not meddle too much in the lives of our grown children and their families. There are some lessons that they need to learn alone. Interfering in the process can have devastating results.

Since I was forced to fight all my life, I took care of my child because he was my responsibility, and no one was going to take that away from me. No one was going to make his life miserable or uncomfortable or hurt him the way my parents did to me. I don't blame my mother for the trauma of my early life. I feel sorry for her, and I became her protector. In the same way, I was going to guard my son fiercely from anyone or anything that even looked as if it would harm him.

In the tenement yard, a woman, Mrs. Harris, lived with her daughter, Hilda, in one of the houses. I was always impressed with Hilda because after graduating high school, she went to nursing school. The family also left an impression on me because of how clean they left the shared kitchen. On Fridays, Mrs. Harris and her daughter fixed their dinner, left their side of the kitchen spotless, and were finished with all the cooking and cleaning before sundown. On Saturday mornings, they would faithfully walk to church.

Because of the Salvation Army's generosity in finding me a place to work and their forgiveness of my sin of having a child out of wedlock, I felt comfortable going back to church there. I appreciated the job they gave me, and I felt as if the church was familiar since I knew most of the people there. However, something inside me was distressed. I felt as if I spiritually lacked something. When Mrs. Harris began talking to me about God and the Bible and the seventh-day Sabbath, I was open and curious.

Views of Kingston where the author lived

In the tenement yard, there was one electric light next to the cistern and the kitchen. Mrs. Harris would lead Bible studies under this light post, and I willingly started attending them. Her lessons were focused on the Bible. I began learning more about the Lord than I ever had before. Sometimes the landlady would shut off the electric light before Mrs. Harris finished teaching, and Mrs. Harris would simply go to her house and bring out a handheld lantern to continue the lesson. Her love for the Lord and her devotion to Him was evident in all her actions. When Mrs. Harris invited me to attend a Sabbath meeting with her, I was eager to try out this new church.

Imagine my surprise when I walked through the door of the North Street Seventh-day Adventist Church on Sabbath morning only to find some of the best-dressed people I had ever seen. With such a tight budget, I could not afford luxuries like new clothes. When the church members came up to talk with Mrs. Harris and me, I could tell they were also well-educated. Instead of feeling as if I fit into this new church, I felt as if the people were snooty and looking down on me. However, I hovered close to Mrs. Harris and was able to get through. I enjoyed her company and teaching so much that I would have happily swum across the ocean if she led the way.

My job was still at the Salvation Army switchboard, but I began regularly attending the SDA church. I talked with Ben about the Sabbath, but neither of us understood it in depth. Eventually, I stopped attending the Salvation Army services. Although the people at North Street SDA scared me, I was learning so much about baptism and Holy Communion, and other important parts of God's Word that I could not pass up the opportunity to learn about God. I also continued attending Mrs. Harris' Bible studies in the tenement yard. My spirit craved the biblical knowledge it had gone so long without, but my shyness and fear kept me from committing to this new faith at first.

Around this time, my mother became ill. She started acting very strange. Whenever she was in her house, she would become violently ill and act weird, but when she was in my house, she was fine. She would not have any recollection of being ill. This went on for a couple of months. When we took her to the doctor, he did not know what was wrong with her. Once, in her state of illness, my mother wandered to the pier and was about to jump off into the ocean. Thankfully, someone saw her and was able to prevent her from committing this action. He brought her home, but we were very worried.

My father then found out from one of his sons that a voodoo curse was placed upon my mother by the son's jealous mother. Although most people associate the voodoo demon-worshipping religion (called "obeah" in Jamaica) with Louisiana and other Caribbean islands, it is prevalent anywhere slaves were brought from Africa. In Jamaica, it is mostly confined to the countryside, but there are several stores that sell items for it in Kingston. It is believed the pagan religion originated in Benin. The word "voodoo" means "spirit," and the religion is practiced by communicating with demons. Like many other pagan religions that have been exposed to Christianity, the practitioners of voodoo claim to worship "god" when, in fact, they are worshiping the devil.

When I talked with Mrs. Harris about my mother, she assured me that God's power was much stronger than the opposition. She got together some other members of the church, and we began to pray first in my house. I had a bottle of olive oil on the table that I used for my baby's skin, and as the prayers got intense, it was as if a hand smashed the bottle off the table across the floor. I can still see in my mind's eye the huge mark it left on the floor. I was never able to remove the mark for as long as I lived there. I was so scared after witnessing that, but the ladies and one gentleman said not to move; just keep on praying. When they were finished, we cleaned up, and then we went down to my mother's house and prayed there. That's where I was ready to grow wings and fly because as we were praying, the house began to shake like an earthquake. The ladies were commanding the devil to get out and go back where he came from, and they were claiming all this in the name of Jesus. I am so glad that God did not look at my fear but counted the prayers of the believers because He knew my knees were shaking as much as the house was.

Then they took my mother to the elders, who anointed her and prayed with her. We were not allowed to go with them. The amazing thing was that my mother knew nothing of her journey to and from the elders. Even today, my mother has no recollection of that experience in her life.

One evening after this event, I was lying on my back across my bed. It was between 3:00-4:00 p.m. My son was playing to my right, and I had my right forearm over my forehead. Suddenly, a heat came over my face, and a blinding light covered my face to the point I could not open my eyes. I heard a voice like thunder that said, "Thelma, come, and come now." You see, I had been back and forth with the idea of the Sabbath and leaving the Salvation Army Church, but I had never discussed it with anyone. When I had that experience, I forgot I had my child on the bed with me. I jumped up and rushed out the door, thinking something was happening. Quickly, after exiting my house, I realized nothing was happening outside of what I had just experienced.

When I told Mrs. Harris about the experience, we both agreed this must have been a message from the Lord. Mrs. Harris felt it was time for me to get baptized.

My baptism was not, however, sincere. A person I respected told me to be baptized, so I was. At the time, it was more like another swearing-in ceremony to me. I began canvassing other neighborhoods with Mrs. Harris, helping her with Bible studies and handing out literature. Ben laughed and told me the Adventists were too "Jewish" for him.

> *"Our Father" and "trust" did not go together in my mind because the only earthly father I had was anything but trustworthy.*

Outside, I was doing the things that made it appear as if I were truly converted and even sticking to the strict SDA dietary requirements, but inside it was different. I now could recognize God's presence in my life, and I understood the direction He was guiding me, but I could not figure out how God could be a loving and trustworthy Father. "Our Father" and "trust" did not go together in my mind because the only earthly father I had was anything but trustworthy.

Once I was baptized, my reoccurring dream about the beautiful meadow and the stream I could not cross stopped. I had finally found that peaceful place I so longed for during my childhood. Although I had not yet discovered how to trust the Lord, I did know that I was on the path to a new life.

God had to show me many miracles and walk beside me through many trials before I finally figured out His love and devotion. It should have been clear from the start. After all, I had witnessed my mother's transformation. It was as if I had witnessed God's power, and that was still not enough. I kept straying from the path and getting stuck in the brambles before I finally realized His way is always best.

Despite my outward dedication to the Seventh-day Adventist biblical teachings, my heart still had a long way to go before I would be ready to take that leap of faith and completely trust the Lord. In addition, I continued allowing Ben to visit me. I know now that God was trying to make me realize that I did not need an earthly man but that He alone could be the solid Rock that would deliver me from poverty and my hopeless situation. Sadly, I had to go through much more in my life before I was truly able to rest in the meadow of my dreams.

Chapter 4

Not surprisingly, I became pregnant with my second child by Ben. When I was pregnant the first time, I was shunned and insulted, but nothing prepared me for the backlash against the second pregnancy.

The Salvation Army had already been expressing their discontent that I was attending Seventh-day Adventist Sabbath meetings. Upon hearing I was pregnant again, I was fired. They said the reason was because I was clearly not sorry about having children out of wedlock. Ben and his parents added fuel to the fire when they told me it was not his child and that I was seeing someone else besides him. Whereas my oldest son had become an accepted grandchild, the new baby growing inside me was completely dismissed as not related to them. When my father heard about this, he took a machete and threatened to chop the family to pieces for insinuating that I was "running around." Since the tenement yard was like living among extended family, he knew that no other male had been over to visit me.

I gave birth to my second son on June 20, 1978. My mother was the first person to step forward and offer me another job at the store she and my father had purchased. I gladly accepted it. After working there for a few weeks, my father found out that my mother was paying me for my work. He was irate. He told her that I would no longer be getting a paycheck since they frequently gave me food. My work in the store, in his eyes, was only to pay them back for the food my son and I ate. I found myself faced with another dilemma. I not only had to take care of myself and one child but two children. I realized that I deserved everything that came to me because God punishes us for our sins. At least, that was my thought process then. I believed that because I sinned after publicly confessing that I had accepted Christ, all the bad things happening to me after that moment were justified punishment for my continued sins. I had a long way to go before I learned about grace and mercy. Because my heart was still occupied with full-blown hate for my father, there was no place for anything else.

Pregnant with 2nd son

Jamaica does not have street-cleaning machines. So, I joined the street sweepers or Corporation, as we called them. This job required me to head out into the streets at 2:00 a.m. each morning and manually sweep them with a broom. Not only did I have to look out for traffic but also criminal activities that occurred during those early morning shifts. The pay was something, but it was not that great. It was honest money to feed my children and me and to pay my rent. God promised He would meet my needs—not provide me riches. He kept me safe during those hours.

I knew sweeping streets would not be a permanent job for me, but it paid the bills until a friend who worked at JAMINTEL recommended a job at Hanna Bros., a motorcycle rental place. I gladly made the transition from early morning sweeper to daytime secretary who kept track of the bookkeeping and motorcycle rentals. I was able to keep my job with them until they closed their doors.

With the second pregnancy and the negative responses I received from others in the Salvation Army Church, I started distancing myself from Ben. Although he had completed his study at the University of the West Indies and worked as a refrigeration and air conditioning technician, he had never proposed marriage or even moving in somewhere together so he could better financially support his growing family and spend more time with his boys. I was getting old enough to realize that he never would.

At my new job with Hanna Bros., I worked with someone who was very kind to me. He talked frequently about how great America was. He had family in America, and he convinced me I could go there to get a fresh start. However, the Lord had different plans for me.

I went to apply for a passport and could not get a copy of my birth certificate from the government. I kept looking for it, but there was no Angela Gordon born on my birthday to my parents. After several searches and talking to my parents, it was at this time in my life that I discovered I was not really Angela, but Thelma! Somehow, my parents could not agree on the name, so when I was registered as Thelma on my birth certificate, my father drew a line through it and wrote in Romana so that I would be named after my aunt. My mother decided she did not like that and drew a line through it and wrote in Angela. All my school records used Angela because I thought that was my name. Once that was resolved, and my passport was finally in hand, I headed off to the embassy to get a visa.

I was so excited when I finally had the most important items I needed to go to America. I could not wait to make plans for my trip, but when I came home, the water main had broken, and the water truck was in the neighborhood supplying water. I rushed inside and set my purse down on the bed with my children and then headed back out immediately to get our drinking water.

When I came back in, the baby was peacefully coloring with a pen from my bag. I was shocked when I discovered his coloring book was my passport and the newly acquired visa. It was all completely ruined. I realized that was a sign this was not the right time for me to go to the United States.

I stopped attending church around this time. I did not want to have to face the stares of the people at the Seventh-day Adventist Church, so I simply stopped going. As I drifted away from church, my co-worker and I began spending more time together. I knew I needed a positive male role model for my boys. He not only interacted well with them but he was also kind and thoughtful. Surprisingly, he offered to move me out of the tenement yard and into a nicer neighborhood. He volunteered to pay for the house rent.

Looking around at the violence, drug use, and our living conditions, I decided it was an offer I would not refuse. I wanted my children to see something better and different than I had seen, and so the next thing I knew, I was living in a two-bedroom home in a much nicer neighborhood.

I finally had enough money to take care of my kids. Our needs were met, and I felt as if my life had finally changed for the better.

Then, one day, I stepped off the bus on my way home, and my eyes locked with those of Ben's parents. They were coming out of a house only two houses up from where I lived! As soon as I regained my ability to think, I hurried into my home. I knew they had to live in that house, and now, they knew I was their neighbor, too. My only hope at the time was that Ben was not living with them, but he was.

Drake did not live with me or even offer to move in with me, but he did visit my home. The first time Ben saw Drake coming over to my house, he was angry. In all the years I had known him, and after having two children with him, he had never even mentioned or hinted he was considering marriage to me, but somehow, he believed that I should remain loyal to him for the rest of my life. Although I had seen that kind of abusive relationship with my parents, I was no longer willing to walk in the footsteps of my mother.

Despite the fact that Ben had made no legal claim on me as a wife, he came over to my house and forced his way into my home as soon as Drake left. He began hitting me and accusing me of moving next door to him, but I now knew that all men were not abusive to women. The relationship with Drake made me realize that this did not have to occur in adult relationships. I did not have to be someone's punching bag. I had finally had enough.

In America, the machete seems like some brutal foreign weapon that is only useful for hacking through rough jungle or killing people. This is not the way most Jamaicans view it. In Jamaica, the machete is a useful tool that every household owns. Although it is used as a weapon, it is also used as a kitchen knife, for carving wood, to do yard work, to split coconuts, as a paddle for spanking children, and to prepare food for animals.

As I was fleeing Ben's abuse in my home, I managed to grab my machete and turn the tables on him. However, I was not planning to use it to simply hit him with the flat side. At that time in my life, the desire to kill my father for what he had done to me was still burning strong in my heart, and my new desire was to kill this man, who did not seem to care if he hurt me physically and who had crushed my dreams of a happy family and caused me much ridicule as a single mother.

I chased Ben into the street and all the way to his yard with it. As I stood outside screaming at him to never touch me again while waving the machete menacingly, I also threatened to burn down his parents' house. Whether he learned his lesson from the new discovery that I was not some mouse to be trodden upon or whether he began to fear me, I have no idea. From that day forward, he never physically hurt me again. If we saw each other in the street, we made sure that one of us would cross to the other side so we would not have to be next to each other. Today, we are great friends. We have come to know the Lord in a new way, and old things have passed away. Behold, all things have become new!

Chapter 5

It was election time again. Although elections were scary in the tenement yard, they were even scarier in the area where my new home was. By this time, the parties and their elected officials had formed alliances with several Jamaican gang leaders. The politicians would look the other way while the leaders sold drugs and traded rifles and other weapons.

That particular area was an area affiliated with the PNP. So, JLP supporters flocked there just looking for a reason to kill citizens. The buses were especially notorious battlegrounds. You did not want to move because you did not want to draw attention to yourself. I remember one time I sat so still on the bus that the heater burned my leg, but it was much better to have a burned leg than to be shot.

The politicians would look the other way while the leaders sold drugs and traded rifles and other weapons.

It was also scary inside my own home at night. The kids and I would not turn on the lights at all. Bedtime was moved up to sunset. Houses that had their lights on became beacons inviting trouble and violence. I would get both my boys ready for bed, and we would go into my room and lay on the floor. If we heard gunshots, we would not get up to look and see what was happening or whose house was being shot at. If either of my children or if I had to go to the bathroom after we lay down, we would just go right there on the floor. In the morning, there would be extra cleaning, but at least we would be alive.

Because of the poor economic situation in Jamaica, the motorcycle shop where I worked closed. Drake found a new job, but it was uptown and further away from my home. He helped me find a new job and also rented a new home for me closer to where he worked.

The new, posh home had three bedrooms, a living room, a nice kitchen, and a backyard with mango trees, and a shed. For the first time in my life, I even had a telephone. Since the boys were older, Drake not only continued paying the rent on my home but also paid so the boys could go to a private Catholic School.

When I moved out of the tenement yard, I did miss Mrs. Harris and her daughter as neighbors. At the time of this move, I was relieved to be moving away from Ben. Still, with all the things Drake gave me and paid for, he never asked me to marry him or asked if he could move in with me. I felt uncomfortable about our situation, but I never pressed him about it. Without being reminded in Sabbath meetings that I was sinning, I could easily ignore my conscience on the matter. After watching him with my children and seeing how kind he was to me, it was easy to imagine that if I waited long enough, he would marry me, and we would live happily ever after.

Not attending Sabbath meetings with Mrs. Harris had taken its toll in other parts of my life as well. I abandoned the Adventist diet completely. The market was now within walking distance of my new home. This meant I would head out on the Sabbath to look at the wares. Again, my conscience bothered me, but I hushed it. After all, I finally had everything I needed, so why would I bother seeking the Lord's will for my life?

Local Market

Although I had moved away from Ben and his family, I continued to take my kids to see their grandparents. I also kept in contact with Ben's kind sister. Unfortunately for their family, Ben's father was a gambler. When he lost his job, he kept gambling, and this put the family in financial trouble. After years of financial comfort, they could no longer pay their bills. One day, Ben's sister told me they were about to be kicked out of their home and would have to live on the streets.

This took me by surprise, but I could not bear to let them suffer in a way that might endanger their lives even though they had caused my children and me years of suffering. So, I told her they could all stay with me until they got back on their feet as long as Ben was not with them.

Not surprisingly, they accepted my offer and lived with me for six months. This was an awkward time. None of us talked to each other. They would buy their own food, but they never offered to pay me any rent. Even after they left my home, they continued storing things in my shed free of charge.

It was during this time that my refrigerator broke down, so I went out to the shed and began using their stored refrigerator. Ben needed the refrigerator but never stopped to think it was benefitting the boys, so he came and took it. I had to store my food in our neighbor's fridge until I could finally afford a new one.

I knew living my life the way I was meant I was living outside of God's will. Eventually, my conscience could not be quieted any longer. I started hinting about marriage, but Drake always avoided the subject. Although my conscience was not at ease, I enjoyed my current lifestyle for the sake of my children. I could not bear to think about returning to the tenement yard and the life of not knowing how I would provide for them, so I did not press the issue with him. I continued to bury the unease that kept building inside me about our relationship. Then, one day, I tried calling Drake, and another woman answered the phone. A sinking feeling hit me like a rock. *Was Drake really the doting man I thought he was?* I might have been able to numb my conscience enough so that I could continue a relationship with a man who was not married to me, but I certainly did not want to be a second or third woman to any man.

The memory of my own father and his infidelity flooded over me. The first man I chose beat me like my father did. Now, this man kept women just like my father. I remembered my father's other children wandering over to our home at different times. There were so many that my mother and I could never keep all of them straight. I wondered if I could be happy even if Drake married me but still kept other women all over the city.

Chapter 6

My mind swirled. If I confronted Drake, I could lose everything and end up in the tenement yard again, or Drake could turn violent and begin physically abusing me. It was then I decided that I was done with life in Jamaica. I had heard so much about the United States that I finally decided to go on a trip and see if everything I had heard were true. I gathered up my paperwork and went back to the embassy to apply for another visa. I was successful. This time I guarded the visa carefully.

Before leaving, I had my mother move into my home. There, she could care for my children while I was away, clearing my head. I told her not to allow Ben to take them even for visits. I was afraid if he found out I was away, he might try to take them away from me permanently.

I had an uncle living in New York, so he and his wife allowed me to stay with them during my time in the United States. While I was there, I decided I would confront Drake. I began asking about his family living in America and where they lived. During our phone calls, I constantly pressured him to marry me when I returned. Finally, after I had asked him yet again why we could not get married, he admitted he was already married but in the process of a divorce. That was all it took for me to hear God closing the gates of heaven and sealing my fate. In my mind, I had committed an unpardonable sin. I decided God had washed His hands of me. I completely ended my relationship with Drake. Surprisingly, he understood and continued to visit the boys and my mother. He made sure their needs were taken care of in Jamaica while I used up my savings living with my uncle and his wife as I filed for residency status. Soon, my greatest fears were realized. Ben had shown up at my Jamaican home, and my mother was unwilling to stand up to him. He took my children to his mother, which meant I had to start sending money to her instead of allowing my mother to take care of them. As if that were not injury enough, he also took some of my furniture. The worst part was that my youngest son was going to be around a family who had never accepted him. My heart was broken into thousands of pieces all at once.

The first step to US citizenship was my Green Card (US resident status). As soon as I received my Green Card, I began filing so my children could come to America. Having my Green Card also gave me the ability to work legally. I wasted no time getting a job at the Martin E. Segal Company (now the Segal Group).

At the interview, the lady asked me what I saw myself doing ten years in the future. I was confident when I told her I would be a supervisor by then. She was aghast. She replied that she had been there ten years and was only a senior secretary for her boss, Mr. Jiggs. Despite my optimism, she hired me anyway as a word processor.

The Martin E. Segal Company was primarily involved in developing employee benefit plans. These included health programs and, by the time I worked there, retirement programs. I learned as much as I could about my work and did it to the best of my ability, never losing sight of my goal to become a supervisor. Even Mr. Jiggs noticed my dedication and frequently complimented me on my skills. My hard work paid off, and I was moved to the Actuary Department. There, I was in line to become a senior secretary to one of the actuaries.

This is where my life took yet another turn. The computer revolution was in full swing, and the World Wide Web was just about to be invented. It was at this point that the Martin E. Segal Company invested in the state-of-the-art Gateway computers that had recently taken the United States by storm. The Gateway computers allowed us to dive into networking and greatly improve our efficiency. The problem was that the technology was new, and no one at Martin E. Segal understood it completely.

With my eagerness to constantly improve myself, I dove into learning the system. I worked so hard that I was one of five chosen to go to a special school to further my networking education. When I completed the school and returned to my position, I was then asked to create a manual that would help others learn what I had. I also created the help desk.

After work, I would still return home to my uncle's house. My uncle's wife had two daughters, and we would party together every weekend. I was exposed to parties in their home as well as being invited to parties outside the home, where I would be the designated driver.

At the time, I felt as if I were on top of the world with all the money and nightlife anyone could want. Looking back on this time, I see myself sinking to the bottom of a pit. I was meeting many new people, and we were having "fun," but inside, I was empty. I did not have my children. I did not have a husband. I was working hard, sometimes doing three jobs at once, but that hard work was not glorifying the Lord. Instead, my money was being saved up and sent to Jamaica to people that I felt were not doing right by my boys. At the same time, I was saving up for the day they would finally come to be with me.

Depressed over the situation with my children and the meaninglessness of a life without the Lord at its center, I stumbled into another bad relationship. This time, I made sure he did not have a wife, but that did not mean I found out everything important about him. Not surprisingly, I became pregnant a third time.

With two bad relationships behind me, I do not know what made me think this third one would be any better. I finally moved out of my uncle's house into a basement apartment. I was not involved in church at all, and it showed in the poor choices and the way I conducted my life. All bad choices, though, have bad consequences. This particular relationship ended up in a disaster that could have catapulted me into something I would never have been able to recover from outside of the hand of God.

At that moment, I realized that I could not travel through life alone, depending on my own choices and judgments. Trusting my earthly father was impossible, but why did I continue trusting these other earthly men who all let me down? It seemed to me the more I looked at my life, the more I realized the only peace I had was when I attended the North Street Seventh-day Adventist Church with Mrs. Harris as my spiritual guide.

I have to say at this point that there might be someone reading this book who has already passed judgment and categorized me and others with similar experiences like my own, but I would simply say to them what Jesus said, "He that is without sin among you, let him throw a stone at her first" (John 8:7).

I longed to return to the safety of the church so badly that I asked one of my friends where I could find the nearest SDA church. She pointed me in the direction of the church. I prayed, "God, I don't know how I am going to do this, but I need to get back on the path. I am lost, and I don't want to live this way anymore. I need to come back to you!" I heard a whisper to open the book of Zechariah to chapter 4, verse 6. I had never read it before. There I found, "Not by might nor by power, but by My Spirit, Says the LORD of Hosts" (Zech. 4:6).

That Sabbath, I put on my nicest red winter dress, black boots, buttoned up my coat tightly because it was beastly cold, and began the walk to the church. In Jamaica, churches are all over. My walk to the SDA church with Mrs. Harris was less than half a mile.

Prayer

In New York, things were a little different. I had to walk one to two miles to get to the SDA church. Upon my arrival, I was saddened to discover no one was there.

I returned home and called my friend. I thought maybe she had made a mistake. Perhaps the church had even moved. My friend insisted that there was a church there and people still attended meetings. At around 9:15 a.m., I completed my second morning walk to the church. It was still extremely cold, and still, there was no one around to welcome me into the building. I returned home, but I did not want to give up. I decided I would keep walking to the church and checking for people. Finally, I arrived to find people. A woman named Sarah was the first to greet me. She radiated warmth, vibrancy, and love. It felt as if I had finally come home.

> *God had been leading me from a child on a journey into His remnant church. I took some detours by the choices I made, but He never left my side.*

Sarah and I became instant buddies, and she mentored me in the same way Mrs. Harris initially mentored me. I longed for that kind of fellowship! I began spending time with her in her large home. She had so many books that I would get lost in her library.

One of the first times I visited her home, I was looking through some of her books, and one fell off the shelf. As I leaned over to pick it up, I noticed it was opened to a familiar picture. It was the picture I loved in the book I looked through as a child with the falling stars. When I picked up the book, I looked at the title and discovered it was Smith's *Daniel and the Revelation*. Seeing that picture and the book I loved as a child made me realize I was finally on the right path. God had been leading me from a child on a journey into His remnant church. I took some detours by the choices I made, but He never left my side. He carried me some of the way, and other times, He walked beside me. Seeing that picture made me realize I was finally home. I decided to re-dedicate my life and be re-baptized, only this time it was from my heart.

Chapter 7

My last son was born April 22, 1989. With such a warm welcome at the church, I quickly realized that the Lord was the One who had been missing from my life. My new church was like home, and all the people in it were like family. It was vibrant and had many ministries for singles, single parents, couples, and young people. There was never a dull moment.

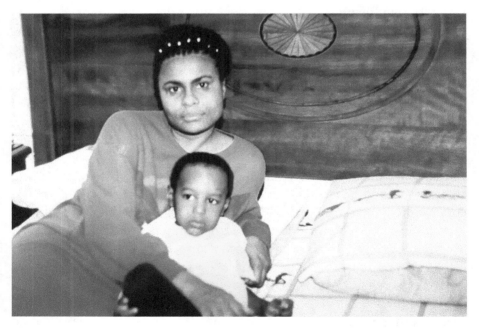

Author with youngest son in New York

In addition to Sarah, I met other people, including Robert Nicholls. The more we spent time together, the more we grew as friends. Robert had been previously married and had one daughter. We first got to know each other when the church set up a prayer partner program. Robert and I were paired and began spending time together as we prayed.

I learned how to pray more effectively with Robert at my side. As Robert and I prayed each morning, we realized we had so much to talk about. Since Robert had been divorced, talking about it was an outlet for him. I remembered talking to his ex-wife about reconciling, but I soon realized that was not going to be possible. Instead, we prayed and left it at that.

Robert, Sarah, and I were good friends. We could talk for hours without missing a beat. Robert and Sarah loved my son, Gregory, so much and helped me with him. It seemed Robert, especially, spent more time with my little baby than I did. He would pick him up from the sitter and take care of him before I got home from work.

As we continued to spend time together, we found we had so much in common that we wanted to spend even more time together. Robert started buying me gifts. We waited for each other after work so we could take the train together. We also worked out at the same gym.

Spending time with Robert was refreshing, but the thought of anything beyond our close friendship burdened my heart. The weight of my past mistakes fell heavily upon me. One day, Robert asked me to accompany him to a store to purchase a ring for his sister in Barbados. At the time, his sister and I were the same size. He said she wanted me to fit the ring because she felt if it would fit me, it would fit her. I agreed. He asked my opinion about the style and quality. I helped him choose what I thought was a beautiful ring.

The following week, I was ill and had the day off from work. Robert came home and proposed to me with the same ring I had chosen. He confessed he had tricked me into picking out my own ring. By that time in my life, I was hardened by the disappointments, hurts, failures, and everything else that I had been through. I responded by telling him to get off his knees and stop talking nonsense. I was feeling ill, so he placed the ring on my finger as I lay in bed.

I felt the weight of all my past sins on my shoulders. My bad track record with men did not give me any confidence. I did not believe I could say "yes" to someone who would actually love and cherish me as well as place God first in our relationship. I was very worried that after all my previous mistakes, this would just be another bad relationship to add to the list. I did not want to marry Robert only to discover he was too good to be true. When we came together to pray after Robert's proposal, we also prayed that God's will would be done in the matter of the special relationship that had developed between us.

Over time, the Lord opened my eyes and made me realize that Robert was much different from anyone in my past. The biggest difference was the way I took time to get to know Robert without beginning a relationship that might have blinded me to imperfections or vice. Another difference I could see was that Robert was proposing marriage instead of running away from it. He was a practicing Seventh-day Adventist Christian and desired to obey God. He helped with Gregory and supported my work to bring my other children to the United States. Most of all, he kept me laughing. I enjoyed every moment with him around. Sometimes, I would get a stomachache from laughing with him. After much prayer and consideration, Robert's constant reassuring presence, I finally agreed to marry him.

Almost a year had passed since I sent Ben's mother the papers that would enable my children to immigrate. I knew the system was slow, but I began to get anxious. I started calling government agencies to find out how much longer it would be and what was delaying the process. At this point, I made another shocking discovery: according to immigration, Ben's mother never filled out the required paperwork and turned it in to them. They had received my paperwork and responded by mailing paperwork out to her. Since she did not respond, my children had remained in Jamaica unnecessarily for months. I was livid, but again, God's plans operate on His timeline, not ours. Thankfully, I was able to explain the situation to the immigration office. They allowed me to pick up the process where she had left off, and things began moving quickly.

The wedding date was set for August 26 and August 27 was the date immigration set for me to get my kids. Setting a date for that event did not lessen the stress of the situation. Now, not only was I planning to reunite with my children, but I also found out that my mother and father were both extremely ill in Jamaica. Despite her health problems, my mother wanted to come to my wedding, so there were travel plans to be made. Robert and I needed to find a home for our new family—one that would be large enough to hold my children and my parents. Finding a home on that scale in a safe New York City neighborhood close to our church was not an easy task.

Neither Robert nor I liked the tall apartment buildings in the city. Instead, both of us chose to rent single-family basement apartments. These usually were larger than regular apartments and also had their own entrances. Many were located in historic brownstone buildings. Not having to worry about being trapped in an elevator with a strange man was only one benefit I found with the basement apartment. In addition, the giant apartment buildings always felt clustered and tight. Since I had grown up in a one-bedroom home that was also small, many bad memories were triggered by these buildings.

With our family growing, we needed to go from a simple one-room apartment to a four-bedroom apartment. Four bedrooms would allow us enough space for all the children and my parents, but this was impossible to find in a basement apartment, especially on our budget. We were looking all over the city and finally found a two-bedroom, basement apartment that was within our budget, but it was obviously too small for everyone. We kept praying. The best advice I can give other Christians is to find a group of praying men and women and stick together. Even though we were the youngest in our prayer band, those ladies lifted us up on wings of prayer!

After much prayer, someone told Robert about a house that was for rent. I was skeptical that we could afford a house that would be big enough and in good condition, but this one was within our budget. It had three bedrooms and much more space than the apartment. In addition, we wouldn't have to worry about the legal implications of trying to fit too many people in an apartment.

The house was beautiful! It had everything I dreamed about for a home, and even the fresh carpet was done in the burgundy color I loved. Once we finished looking at the house, we prayed right there in the middle of the living room for God to make a way for us to get it if it was His will for us to have it. As far as we could see, it was perfect, but we knew God can see what we cannot. We had the one hundred dollars needed for the deposit, but the landlady who was supposed to take the money was not there. We were very disappointed that we could not immediately secure the home since it was ideal for us.

Finding a good place to live in New York City on a tight budget is difficult. The housing market is very small, even with all the huge apartment buildings. When you do not want to live in some of the larger buildings, it reduces your choices and the chances of finding anything.

With only one hundred dollars, we could only afford to put a deposit down on one place—the apartment or the house. Robert could come back and try to meet with the landlady to put the deposit down the next day, but we both knew a house like this would quickly find tenants. At the same time, we were concerned about losing the apartment. We could immediately place the deposit on that in order to secure it, but if we waited, we might lose that place as well. After realizing that waiting to place a deposit anywhere could leave us homeless, we went ahead and put the one hundred dollars we had down on the apartment.

This did not mean we gave up on the house. We continued praying about it, even though we did not have the money for a second deposit and even though the apartment had been secured. We would lose the one-hundred-dollar deposit on the apartment if we changed our mind. We prayed that God would open the door and give us the money we needed if He wanted us to have that house. Then we left it in His hands.

In the midst of house hunting, I was also planning our wedding. I went to the cake shop the next morning to pick out our cake, and while I was standing there, I noticed a one-hundred-dollar bill on the ground. I picked up the money and asked the lady behind the counter if she remembered which customer came into the shop before I did. I told her the person had dropped a large sum of money. The cake shop lady insisted that no one had been in the shop before me. I was the first person to come into the shop. She told me that I must have dropped the money, and even if I had not dropped it, the money was mine now. I took that as a sign that God was giving me the money so that we could now put a deposit down on the house. Even if we lost the money for the apartment, this money would replace it.

I told Robert about the gift from the Lord, and we went to pay for the deposit on the house. When we arrived, the landlady stated the house had already been rented out to some girls. Robert and I both believed the Lord wanted us to have the house instead of the apartment and tried to explain

"Whatever you did and whatever you told your God, He answered.

this to the landlady. We even told her about the miracle of the money appearing. She stated that there was nothing we could do short of divine intervention because the girls not only had paid the deposit but also had already arranged for the utilities to be placed in their names. Robert and I knelt and prayed right there, with the landlady watching. We asked God to work things out so that we could have the house if it were still in His will.

Three days later, we were preparing to sign the lease papers on the smaller apartment. As we headed out the door to sign the papers at 6:00 p.m., the phone rang. It was the landlady who owned the house.

"I don't know what you did," she said. "Whatever you did and whatever you told your God, He answered. Those girls came back and told me they changed their minds. They took their names off the utilities. The house is now available if you want to come and put the deposit on it. I figured I would give you the chance to do it before I put it back on the market."

As soon as we got off the phone with her, we called the people who were waiting for us to sign the lease on the apartment and told them we would not be coming because we had found another place to live. Once the appointment was canceled, we took the deposit directly to the landlady for the house. We may have originally wanted a four-bedroom home, but the three-bedroom home was just the perfect size for our family and my parents when they came for the wedding.

Planning the wedding, finding a new place to live, arranging for my children to come live with us permanently, and making plans for my mother to come to the wedding was a lot of work all at once. Robert knew what my father had done to me as a child, and he was very nervous about allowing this man into his house. However, with my renewed faith, I had finally learned to trust the Lord. I wanted to share my faith with my parents before it was too late. If they lived in our home, not only would I be showing them how a God-loving family lived, but I would also be able to encourage them to live godly lives. I also could provide them with healthy food that would help their ailments. I wanted to truly honor my mother and father as set forth by the Lord.

Author with Second Son on a Jamaica Beach

Finally, the wedding day arrived on August 26, 1990. Both my parents attended, and I was so happy I could finally share that moment with my mother. My wedding day was the happiest day of my life. I had finally found a God-fearing man who loved me for whom I was and not for what he could get out of me. Sadly, Robert's ex-wife would not let his daughter attend the wedding, and my children were still in Jamaica.

The very next day, I got on the flight I had booked to Jamaica. After three long years of paperwork and phone calls, my kids were finally coming to their new home in the USA.

Chapter 8

Unfortunately, everything remained difficult, even after marrying Robert and bringing my children home. My father was extremely ill from his life of excess. Shortly after arriving here, he had to go to the hospital. He was diagnosed with peripheral vascular disease. All the years of smoking marijuana and tobacco had caused plaques to build up in his blood vessels, making the passageway smaller and harder. With smaller blood vessels, less oxygen got to his legs. Some of the tissue in his hands and feet died without it. This led to gangrene in one of his legs, and it had to be amputated.

My mother was also in poor health to the point where she looked sickly at my wedding. Thankfully, her health conditions were mainly related to living in poverty and not getting the proper diet. When she also ended up in the hospital, I went down to fill out the paperwork for both my parents to stay in the United States. I also used my knowledge of healthy living to help repair her health.

As my husband expected, living with my father under the same roof was more difficult than I imagined. Not only did I fear daily that he would enter my room while I was getting dressed or he would grab me as I walked past him, but I also had not yet forgiven him. Here was the man I hated—the man I had once planned on killing—and I had to now care for him and my mother. Having him in the same house was too close and created tension throughout. Still, I felt it was my duty to honor my aging parents by attending to their health needs.

My husband was not only worried about me but was also uncomfortable with the situation. Even though I did eventually forgive my father in 1992, my husband continued to struggle with what had happened to me and with the man who did it. For me, forgiveness released a giant weight from my soul. The anger and hatred had consumed me and affected my relationship with God. By turning my past over to Him, I was able to move forward with my life. In addition, I wanted to witness to my parents. One of the rules I set up in the house was that as long as they were living with me, they had to come to church with us. They accepted this condition, but I knew I needed to show how being a Christian changed my life and could also change theirs. As long as I harbored the resentment, I could not effectively do that.

While I was dealing with the relationship I had with my parents, living in the same household as my father, and resolving the emotional turmoil I suffered, I also had to deal with new family dynamics as my two older children found themselves with a new father, new little brother, and a new stepsister in a new country.

On that front, the situation between my husband and children was cold. My oldest, especially, struggled in his new family. He had been raised by Ben's parents, who adored him. Robert was a new male figure in his life, and he did not have any respect for him. Although my children were never rude, they did not have the loving relationship I hoped they would have with Robert. In part, this distance developed because of the adjustment issues my children had to living in a new country, in a new family, and with a new school.

Jamaica has an entirely different school system that is based on the British school system since it was once a British colony. When the children came here, they had to get used to an entirely different way of teaching. The oldest had the most trouble adjusting. By the time he was fifteen, one year after he had come to the USA, he had been in a lot of trouble with the schools. There were many times we thought he was attending school only to find out he had skipped and played video games all day. This caused him to get further behind in school. By the time he was sixteen, he had decided he would drop out.

Since I had not been able to complete my schooling, I studied hard and earned my GED. I felt as if I had overcome a big milestone. All those years in Jamaica when I wanted to learn but was not allowed to go to school were finally behind me. The GED was not only a stepping stone to higher education but also a goal in itself. I was working and raising three kids, but I managed to set aside the time to study for the test.

Church was something else that the kids had to adjust to attending. While I lived with them in Jamaica, I had not attended meetings since shortly after my second child was born. When my sons lived with my mother, they also never attended church. It was only when they began living with Ben's mother that they started regularly going to church, and it was the Salvation Army church. The oldest started playing trumpet in the Salvation Army band. The informal services had made my children see church more as a social outlet instead of a place to draw closer to the Lord and learn about His way.

The relationship with Robert's daughter was another difficult situation. She loved Robert and wanted to spend more time with him. Her mother, however, was still bitter over their divorce. She did all she could to prevent the relationship between Robert and his daughter from growing. When I tried to encourage the relationship, she would lash out at me. However, these are troubles any family will have when trying to repair a broken home.

Chapter 9

As I grew in the Lord, I wanted to volunteer more at church. Robert and I were involved with the youth, the eldership, and several outreach projects in the communities. As we stepped forward to help where needed, it seemed there was always more work that needed to be done. In one case, this caused a serious problem.

The church clerk at one of the churches we were in had been in that position for years. She was a founding member. With all that Robert and I were doing, I was nominated for that position, and I ended up accepting it. When she found out that I would be taking over as church clerk, she cursed me out. Our relationship declined from there. It even got to the point where she said that she was going to shoot me. I did not know why she was so angry with me. I certainly did not want to take someone's job away from them if they were that attached to it.

At that point in time, the eAdventist.net system had not yet been created. All the churches still kept handwritten records, and that clerk would not give me the church books. The eAdventist.net system has made things much easier for churches and conferences that have signed up for it. If there is a change of clerks, the conference clerk simply creates a new online account for the new church clerk. Since individual clerks no longer house the information in their homes, there is no need to physically transfer the records from one person to another. Once the conference clerk sets up your account, you have access to the records.

However, the only way for me to get the records then was for her to hand them over to me. At first, I simply prayed she would have a change of heart. But as time went on, I had certain things I needed to report and keep track of within the church. Her stubbornness prevented me from doing my job. I figured it was better for her to continue doing the job than for me to fail at doing it because I did not have the necessary records.

I called one of my friends in the church to talk with her about declining the position for the sake of peace. I wanted to see if allowing her to continue with the position would make her feel better and reduce the stress of the moment. Since I had no idea how I was going to keep church records when I did not have the membership records and information created by her, this seemed like my only option. While I was dialing the phone, I heard a voice that said, "This is My work. You have consulted everyone else. How about talking to Me?" I immediately hung up the phone. God used another miracle to show me that He had a plan for me, and if I trusted Him to lead, He would make my feet like hinds' feet.

Instead of focusing on how uncomfortable the confrontation with this clerk was for me, that voice made me begin to think about the whole picture. She was upset at having the position she desired taken away from her, but perhaps the Lord was trying to teach both of us something. A majority had elected me to perform that role. That God wanted me to take over was suddenly obvious.

> *I heard a voice that said, "This is My work. You have consulted everyone else. How about talking to Me?"*

At the same time, I had no desire to create conflict with her. I pondered different ways I could get the church records. I began to recognize that this teaching moment was clearly difficult for her. I am sure to her those records represented her life's work. In her eyes, I was taking the position she believed to be only hers. I was asking her to surrender the records she had worked so hard to complete into my possession, and this was clearly causing her severe emotional distress.

After much thought, I decided it was not worth the fight to physically take the records. I could go to friends or the eldership to see if they would pressure her to give the books to me, but this would only end up with her becoming even more hurt and angry. My solution was to recreate the books. This caused much more work for me because I needed to go around to every member of the church and interview him or her, but it allowed me to avoid an even more painful confrontation while continuing the work the Lord had given me to do.

Some time later after moving to Florida, my good friend Sarah, who had welcomed me so warmly into the church and into her home, left the SDA church and began worshiping in another denomination, and I did not maintain contact with her. I am still saddened today by the loss of her friendship.

Another area of ministry that my husband and I pursued during this time was work with the homeless. We would go to shelters and lead

Bible studies there. One man, in particular, James, had previously been a member of the Seventh-day Adventist Church but had fallen away from his faith. As we continued ministering to him, we began encouraging him to come to meetings with us. James was interested in attending but had no way of getting to church. We offered him a ride and told him the time we would be there to get him.

Neither my husband nor I thought he would actually make the effort to come, but the next Sabbath, we went to pick him up anyway. We were surprised to see him waiting outside for us without a coat on in the cold weather. Robert realized that James could not afford a coat, but his devotion to returning to the Lord was evident because he did not want to miss his ride to church. Robert gave James his coat so that James would not need to be cold while waiting for us on future Sabbaths.

Bible Study

From that point forward, picking him up and taking him to Sabbath meetings became part of our regular Sabbath routine. After the Sabbath meeting, we would bring him home with us to share Sabbath dinner before returning him to the shelter. Several people expressed concern about bringing a homeless man into our home, but we had seen how serious he was about making a change in his life. Although some people, homeless or not, have a criminal mindset or became homeless because of addictions, some are either down on their luck or struggle with taking on responsibilities because of mental illness. Precaution in any situation is necessary, but it is important to allow the Lord to work through you if you feel called to work with those in need. It is also important not to make judgments based on generalizations.

James is a success story. After witnessing to him and showing him the unbiased love of Christ, he was baptized. He began working for the Lord at the homeless shelter by leading his own Bible studies, and he brought those to whom he witnessed to Sabbath meetings.

In February of 1993, my father died. He was buried in New York. In July of that same year, we felt the Lord calling us to Florida and moved to Orlando to begin a new chapter of our lives.

Thelma and Husband at church in FL

Chapter 10

We moved to Florida in the 1990s, after my father died. It was a difficult decision. Our church family, which was our support system, and our friends were all in New York. I was heavily involved in the youth ministry and other thriving ministries in our church. Life for us began in New York. We really did not know what to expect in Florida, but we went there anyway. We rented a home while we searched for one to purchase. Robert had a cousin already living there, and we felt as if we would have good support as we navigated this new chapter of our life.

In New York, I had started at Martin E. Segal as a secretary and had been trained and quickly promoted to network administrator. So, of course, when we moved to Florida, I expected I would be able to find a job easily. With many prayers and much faith, I submitted my résumés with several applications. It was not long before I began getting interviews. During each interview, the interviewer would always say the same thing—"Sorry, you are overqualified for this position." I began to get frustrated because I did not understand why they had wasted my time with an interview if they felt I was overqualified.

Discouragement set in, so I decided to apply at a temporary staffing agency. Finally, I was hired. The work was not secure, but I was thankful to have an income. The money was not much, but we were able to pay the rent and provide food. In addition, the temp agency would sometimes send me to places that would interview me for more permanent positions. Many of these were bad fits for me, but there was one position at a facility that I really enjoyed. I worked in this position for a long time. As with every job, I attacked it with vigor, learning all I could about it—even implementing some new strategies. I did such a good job that I was assigned to train someone without any previous knowledge or skills for that job. I did not realize I was training someone to replace me.

Shortly after I finished training this new employee, I was called into the supervisor's office, who was an Englishwoman. She presented me with a list of "instances" where I had "made mistakes." I stood there in shock. Everything she was saying about my poor performance was a lie. I was the person who started the system and organized the flow of it. I did not hold anything back and passed all this information onto the new employee. If they felt I was such a "liability to the company," I didn't understand why they wanted me to train someone else. What knowledge did this British woman have on which to base all her alleged errors? I realized my skin made me the odd one out in that office. One of the other employees was friends with the new employee's mother, and they had the correct skin tone.

From the start, it felt as if the environment of the office could not accept or help a "black" woman to grow, so I realized my skin must have been the real basis for the accusations. I told the supervisor I was not going to let her fire me and taint my work record with her unfounded accusations just so she could give her "white" counterpart the job. I told her I would quit instead, but I let her know that I saw her actions as racially motivated. I told her I came there with my knowledge and skills, and I was walking out of there with all of it and then some. With that, I left the office before she could say anything else.

I want to point out here that being a child of God does not exclude us from the evils of this world, neither does it do us any good to ignore the fact that evils do exist by not dealing with them directly. Address it and move on to life's next challenge. God has given us a command to love everyone regardless of evils visited upon us by them.

Robert also struggled with this kind of racial hate in his employment. It was difficult for him to find a place to work. They often said they were not hiring any "niggers." When he did find someone to look past his skin tone and hire him, they would "forget" to pay him sometimes. In many cases, we used my paycheck alone to get through the week. When I lost my job, the small security my income provided was no longer there.

God was right there with us in all our struggles, just as He was with Daniel in the lions' den. While we traveled through these struggles, we asked many questions of God, just as many people do when they are struggling. We wanted to understand why we were going through some of the things we were going through, but we never questioned Him. Asking God to reveal His purpose for the trials you suffer is a normal human reaction. Questioning whether God is just in allowing you to suffer any trials reveals that you need to work on your relationship with and understanding of God as the Sovereign of the universe who holds your life in His hands. Job underwent trials that he did not understand, and

God revealed that He could see things we cannot. We must trust He is navigating things for the best, even though our path lies through stormy seas. We may lose our boat, but we will not be lost.

Our youngest son was now old enough to go to school, and he loved it. Although I was glad the kids were successful in school, I was uncomfortable because it was strenuous to make ends meet. Coming from a life of comfort to living this struggle was difficult to accept. It was during these times that I came to realize that faith in God is not a word we use during conversations. Faith is an action word. It must be demonstrated even when we cannot see or hear God. As it says in Hebrews 11:1, "Now faith is the substance of things hoped for, the evidence of things not seen." We must exercise the faith we have in a Sovereign God, understanding that He will do only what He wills to do because He is Sovereign.

The manager in charge of our rental was a Christian man who understood the hard financial times we were going through. With Robert's sporadic paychecks, sometimes we would have to wait to pay our rent, and it would be overdue. The manager knew we would pay it as soon as we could afford to do it. Despite this, the owner of the property eventually found out that we were not paying on time. Once he did, he told the manager we must be evicted, and we were.

With nowhere to live, a friend from one of Robert's jobs let us park our van by his house. He even offered to let the boys sleep inside the house because he had a spare room. However, he was a smoker, and they had asthma. In addition, I was not about to let my boys sleep in a stranger's house. Instead, the older one slept near his friend's house; the younger one slept in the friend's house, and my mother, the baby, Robert, and I all slept in the van. We went into Robert's work associate's house to use the bathroom. It was not the easiest of situations, but there was nothing else we could do at the time. The first night was strange because as I looked up into the sky through the opening on the side of the van, I was able to see the brightness of the stars, and a sense of peace came over me that I had not felt for a long time. Somehow it felt as if everything was going to be okay.

When Robert's cousin heard about our situation, she gave us enough money to get our own place again. Robert found work out of state, and we found a place to live in Kissimmee. We also transferred to the Kissimmee SDA church. When each job ended, he would look for another out-of-town job because they were more readily available.

In one instance, he was rooming with a man named Mike while on the job. Mike seemed like a nice person, but Robert and he must have started talking about the differences between the North and the South when it came to discrimination. Mike said, "If you think you have met some bad cases, just let me show you how prejudiced my mother is. Here, let me call her."

Robert listened on speakerphone as his roommate dialed the number and greeted her. "Hey, Mom, guess what? I am rooming with a black guy on this job."

"Does he have a knife?" she asked in earnest. "You better hide your money because they are all thieves!"

When Mike hung up, Robert could not believe it. Mike thought his mother was funny, and he could not see the danger in her prejudice. After a little further debate on the issue, Robert finally said, "Think about it, Mike. What if I were arrested for robbery and your mother were on the jury? What if there were six people like your mother on the jury? Do you think I would get a fair trial? What do you think they would do to me whether I was innocent or not?"

It was always my prayer for my children that God would save them and work out His will in their lives.

"I never looked at it that way," Mike replied.

One of the boys got a job at McDonald's to help support himself. With our income only coming in here and there, we had already lost two cars to repossession. Another one of my uncles lived further down in Florida and had a car that he gave to us when he heard we were struggling. This car had a manual transmission. I could not use it since I had never learned to drive one. We decided it would be best used by one of the boys, and so I passed it on to my oldest son. Sadly, he never took care of the car. He would drive it until it ran out of gas or oil, never knowing how to take care of it. There was a golf course across from the home where we lived, and he would go joy-riding across it. His actions tore up the green on the golf course.

He was always trying to find something new and exciting to do, but these adventures cost us more money in the end. He started taking classes at college but did not pay attention and soon dropped out. It seemed that he had no career or long-term life plans that he was dedicated to pursuing. Robert and I were concerned for his future. One day, he walked into the house, grabbed his toothbrush, and told us he had joined the US Marines. We were shocked and worried about the trouble he could get into in the military, but since he was eighteen, he was old enough to make his decisions. It was always my prayer for my children that God would save them and work out His will in their lives. I do not tell God how to do that. If this was God's plan for my son, I was in no way going to intervene with His will.

My second son also began his career working for McDonald's, but he had not struggled with the transition to the American school system as much as my oldest son. When he graduated, he went to college to continue his education, pursuing a degree in computer information technologies. While in college, he managed to get a job at Lucent Technologies, which had recently branched off from AT&T. (It has since undergone several mergers and has now been absorbed by Nokia.) This job provided him with more money than working at McDonald's had. However, it was at night, which cut into his study time. Since he was happy with his new position, he dropped out of college. My children had everything at their disposal to pursue whatever they wanted to do with their lives, and, therefore, I had to respect their choices, though those choices strayed from my vision for them.

During this time, while I was praying and was asking God for guidance and exercising faith, things did not seem to be going in a comfortable direction, but I had a history with God. He had a proven track record that I could follow. I think trusting God's sovereignty is one of the most frustrating things for a Christian. We always want answers to our questions, but God says that some things are His prerogative.

The church had a newsletter where members could publish want-ads and other classifieds. One day, I noticed an ad asking for a typist. The woman posting the ad was writing a book about herbs and their healing powers. However, she needed a typist to finish her project. I knew that my skills as a secretary would be useful, but I did not have a typewriter in order to do the work. When I contacted her and explained the situation, she said she would be more than happy to buy me a typewriter and deduct the cost from my final payment. She asked how much I would charge, but I had never done this kind of work before, so I did not know how much to ask her to pay. She said she would pay me the four thousand dollars to do the job because "out here in California they are charging a lot." I took her word for it and accepted the job. When I finally met her, she was such a sweet person. She was ninety-two but strong as a rock and doing everything for herself: painting, cooking, driving. She even got married while she employed me!

Chapter 11

The part-time job of typing that manuscript did not change my desire to become a nurse that had begun when I was a younger girl in Jamaica. I knew when I was done typing, I would be back to searching for another job, but I did not think the income from the book would help enough so that I could attend college. I decided to check into tuition programs that one of the colleges had available. When I did, I found out that I could get scholarships and tuition assistance for the nursing program, but I first had to pay the pre-registration fees that would cover my books. These fees totaled three hundred eighty dollars. Although this was only a fraction of the cost of attending the school, I could not afford that.

Like always, I decided to go to the Lord in prayer about the situation. I prayed, "Please, Lord, if you find the money for me to pre-register, I will go to nursing school, finish it, and become a nurse for Your glory." I did not get an immediate answer, but I kept praying. The time passed, and the date for classes to start kept getting closer. Finally, it was the Sunday before classes started, and there was a knock on the door. When I opened it, imagine my surprise to see Mrs. Hazel standing there.

"Hello, dear," she said. Before I could invite her into the house, she continued, "The Holy Spirit told me that you needed this." She handed me an envelope.

"You can't pay me," I responded, "because I haven't turned over any work to you yet."

"When God tells me to do something, I don't argue with the Holy Spirit," she said, and she turned around and left. I opened the envelope, and there was money in it. Puzzled, I counted the money, and it was EXACTLY three hundred eighty dollars—the amount I needed for all the pre-registration fees. Through this miracle, God again pointed me in the direction He wanted me to go. The very next day, I went down to the college, paid for my nursing classes, and started the prerequisites for the nursing program.

My older two boys were now independent. The youngest, who was always an easy-going child, did well in school. His life was not always a smooth one, though, and there were challenges with him. He attended an SDA school at this time. I remember him coming home and asking me why his skin was so dark. He wondered why he could not be like the rest of the kids. At the same time, his teachers told us he was having trouble understanding certain things. Hindsight has taught me to listen and pay attention to my children differently. His early life had not been marked with the same changes and challenges that my older boys experienced, so he dealt with things in different ways.

Going to nursing school while my husband was in another state was difficult. This was compounded by the fact that I still had a young child in the home. It was somewhat of a comfort for me to have my mother living with us, but it also came with its own set of ordeals. There were many prayers that God answered for me during that first year.

After feeling as if my life were on the way to something better, I was hit with a setback. Toward the end of my first year in nursing school, one of the long-standing nursing instructors called me in for an interview with her. She told me she did not know why I was in the nursing program and that I needed to choose a different major.

I was confused. I had done well in all of my classes. I told her I was in the nursing program because I wanted to become a nurse. She did all that she could in that interview to persuade me to change my major. At that point, a change would have been financially unwise since I had spent so much time working on a nursing degree and was already in the nursing program. None of the classes I had taken would have easily transferred to a different major. In addition, none of the other majors touched my heart the way nursing did.

I could not tell if this woman was trying to test me to see how strong I was or if this was just another case of discrimination I was running into in Florida. I decided that regardless of her motives, I needed to trust in the Lord to get me past this roadblock. No matter what she told me, I would not back down. I wanted to be a nurse. God had given me the money so I could study to become one. I would not let Him down. I promised Him I would stick with it if He provided the means to do it. After what seemed like a long debate, I left the interview feeling unsettled, but my major had not changed. I was still in the nursing program since she had no academic grounds to dismiss me from it.

The next year, she made my life miserable. In each class I had with her, I was destined to do poorly in it. She would criticize my work to the point I was nervous just sitting down in class. I would turn in papers and receive poor grades without understanding why I had been marked down.

I had two study partners, Kourtney, who was a Caucasian American, and Tehara, who was a Muslim. We all got along well and would frequently work together on projects. We would often talk about how difficult the instructor was and the unfair way it seemed she singled me out from others in the class.

I began to suspect the interview had been more than just a simple vetting of students but rather to weed out the three blacks who were in the program. There were only one or two other African Americans admitted to the program. Sometimes I would get out of lab and head to class only to have the instructor send me back to the lab. As soon as I returned to the lab, I would get in trouble for being there when I was not supposed to be there. The supervisor seemed to constantly find things wrong with what I was doing in and out of class.

As I shared my troubles with my study partners, Kourtney brushed it off. I would tell her I felt the instructor was discriminating against me and that she judged my work by my skin tone instead of by its merit. Kourtney had not experienced any of the issues that I had. She got along well with the instructor and generally got good grades in her class. She could not accept that a nursing supervisor would discriminate in this era. She believed it was just my perception.

Tehara, on the other hand, had also felt the negative attitude of the supervisor toward her. Although she did not have the depth of problems I was experiencing, she was willing to believe the attitudes were more than just perception. Despite how much Tehara and I tried to convince Kourtney of the different treatment, she did not believe us since the discrimination was not happening to her.

The hardest part was when I would submit my nursing care plans that were closely based on the textbook examples, and my supervisor would give me a low grade or make me re-do them completely. I did not receive consistent, constructive feedback that would help me to create care plans the way she wanted them. It was very frustrating. Kourtney thought there was something I was missing in them and wanted to help me find the answer. One day she showed me her nursing care plan—she had received an A on it. We came up with a plan to prove to her that the supervisor was treating me differently. On the next clinical day, I had a patient for whom I could use the same nursing diagnosis that Kourtney used. So, with a few minor changes, such as vital signs, demographics, and other pertinent data and with the omission of one nursing diagnosis, I used the nursing care plan for which Kourtney received an A and submitted it after asking Kourtney to give it a second look. After all, she had received that high grade and knew it met all the requirements because it was very similar to hers.

When I turned in my nursing care plan, I received an F. I was told it was poor work, and the plan was even torn up because the supervisor was so dissatisfied with it. It was only then that Kourtney realized the supervisor had a problem with me specifically. I still was not going to let one person stand between me and my promise to God. I continued praying about the situation and trusted that God would make everything work out in the end because I believed He wanted me to fulfill my dream of becoming a nurse.

At home, our budget was still tight. I think any woman who loves her family will willingly go without food sometimes so they can have something good to eat. That is the choice I made. On the days when I had my nursing clinicals, it was already difficult to stop and eat. I had to be on my feet for the whole day as I rushed around caring for patients. I could not afford to eat outside of the home, so I would go in at 6:00 a.m. without eating breakfast and not eat until I came home at night. We had to carefully budget the money so our son would have lunch money and a good breakfast. We also needed enough money for gas. Sometimes I had to make the choice between breakfast for me or gas for the car. Gas always won. If I didn't have the money or time to eat, I would fill the void in my stomach up with water. Sometimes I would go the whole week on water.

I was also pushing myself in class to do well. I had so much anxiety when I knew I had a class with that particular instructor. Even if I was prepared, it was a struggle, but if I forgot something or if she was in an especially foul mood and felt like making my classroom experience miserable, I would have serious panic attacks. I had to arrange for proctors to give me the nursing tests in the library because I would get too nervous to take the test with her in the same room. These were times I truly experienced God's power. Deuteronomy 33:27 says, "The eternal God is your refuge, and underneath are the everlasting arms." God carried me in His arms.

Going without food under such stressful conditions was bad enough, but I continued demanding more from my body. In order to balance home and school, I needed to stay up late many nights so that I had time to study. I pushed my need for sleep aside. Between the strain and the lack of sleep, I began to lose focus in my daily life.

One day, I had gotten a B on another paper, and I was upset as I drove home. I was so distracted by it that I was not paying attention to anything going on outside of my grade. I did not hear or see that there was a train approaching on tracks I was about to cross. I did not see the rails come down. Thankfully, God's hand woke me from my angry tirade in just enough time to get my car stopped. His miraculous intercession saved my life. As I sat watching the cars pass and reflecting on the fact that I was almost hit by a train over a grade, I asked God for forgiveness. How could I complete my promise to Him if I were no longer alive to do it? As I sat there crying out of sheer weakness, fear, and frustration, I realized I could not hear the train anymore. I did not hear anything but a small voice saying, "I never promised you As and Bs, but I promised that I would see you through it all." I apologized to God, waited for the rails to lift, and drove home in peace.

As I entered my last semester, I tried to keep everything in perspective, but I still pushed myself to the limits. Once, I even had to lean on a patient's bed because I was feeling faint from the neglect I was heaping on my body. I was feeling very unwell, but I did not want to miss clinicals. One absence might give someone a valid reason to declare me unfit for the program, which was a very rigid one.

Finally, the grueling semester was over. Each of us went in to get our grade from the instructor. This time the interview was brief. She told me I had received a B in the course and that I "was going to make a fine nurse."

Author Receiving the Dean's Award in Nursing School

Official Nursing School Graduation Picture

I could not believe it was finished and that she, of all people, would have something good to say about me! I praised God for the good grade, but it was not about the grade. It was about how He kept me throughout the entire ordeal. It was about how He kept my home together and how He kept back the powers of darkness from trying to snuff out my life. It was about how He made my enemy my footstool and how He renewed my strength and mounted me up with eagle's wings. He saw me running and walking amidst the burden, but He never left me alone. Instead, He infused me with His power and strength so much so that I was not weary, nor did I faint. My perseverance was not because of who I am but because of who He is: Jehovah Jireh!

> *I praised God for the good grade, but it was not about the grade. It was about how He kept me throughout the entire ordeal.*

I was forty-two years old when I graduated from the nursing program. I joined the graduating committee and helped plan the ceremony. I was in charge of doing the devotional. It was a proud day when I received my diploma in front of my family, but God was not finished with me yet.

Chapter 12

Immediately after graduating, I got a job at a hospital in Orlando. It was an hour's drive from where I lived, but I was finally getting a regular paycheck. Robert never once complained about having to work two or three jobs to keep things going while I went to school full-time. We weathered the storms together. I could never have asked for a more faithful companion, so after what belonged to God was set aside from my first paycheck, I bought Robert a much-needed suit and shoes for church. Who would have known that when he gave his coat to homeless James back in New York, we would end up experiencing what it was like not having a roof over our heads, too?

That first paycheck, which was the beginning of stable income for us, marked the point in our lives where, like Job, God saw our struggles and devotion to Him through them and once again blessed us more than we could imagine. He began to give us back the years the locusts had stolen from us.

With my new job, we were able to buy what was then my dream home. Although I continued to work in the hospital, I entered a cardiovascular intensive care unit program. When I finished the specialty training, I was able to keep working on that unit. Back then, it was an achievement for me to be placed in an intensive care unit where some of the most critical patients are cared for as soon as I came out of nursing school. I had risen above the fear that plagued me through nursing school, and the teachers I had during the cardiovascular clinicals all complimented my skills. God showed me again that it was not about who or what was outside of me but more about who was inside of me and what He had placed on my heart.

As a cardiovascular nurse, I helped with open-heart surgery. When I witnessed the amazing power in the single organ of the heart, I was blown away. It was so mind-boggling that the only thing I could think about was how our awesome God was so good. Here was this machine made not from inanimate metals and pieced together in such a way that it would break, but a machine made of living cells. An artificial heart made by humans can only last a few years at the most, but the organic, self-sustaining heart that was made by the Lord lasts us a lifetime.

Those who worked on the unit were highly trained. Although all of us had the skills to help anywhere in the hospital that had a code blue, other staff could not help us because of the specialized needs of our patients. Still, being a nurse on the cardiovascular unit was just the next step in my journey to constantly better myself for the Lord. I craved to learn even more. I wanted to know what was causing the patient's problems. Why were certain medications given and not other ones? How did different medications interact? What were the early warning signs to look for in my patients so that I would know how to get them the help they needed soon enough to make a difference? I was constantly seeking answers to my when, why, and how questions.

Being a nurse on the cardiovascular unit meant that I cared for patients who had open-heart surgery. We had a tight schedule to follow. For example, it was our goal on the second day after surgery to get the patient up and help him or her get to the chair in the room to prevent blood clots. Patients who do not get up and move after surgery are at higher risks for pneumonia and other lung problems. Walking actually helps the wound to heal by increasing blood flow.

I could have two patients assigned to me on any given day. One day as I was checking on a patient, his wife came into the room. She walked up to me and told me she wanted to speak with the nurse. I smiled and told her I was the nurse. It was as if this idea was not only new but also incomprehensible to her. Again, she told me to send the nurse into the room so she could talk with her. After a few minutes of trying to explain that she was already speaking with her husband's nurse, the machine for the other patient assigned to me went off. I turned away from her so I could check on the other patient.

While I was away, the first patient began trying to explain to his wife that I was his nurse. The woman refused to believe even him. I decided that nothing was going to make this woman believe that I was a professional nurse in charge of her husband's care. Instead of continuing to try to break through her prejudice, I simply walked back over her side of the room and began talking to her about how her husband was doing. I thought back to all the questions most worried spouses asked me and answered all of them that I could without waiting for her to direct any questions to me.

As soon as I had told her everything that I could think to tell her, I finished by saying, "The doctor will be in soon. If you are unsatisfied with the information I gave you about your husband's condition, you are welcome to bring up your concerns with the doctor directly, but you will have to wait until he makes his rounds."

At that point, I did not wait for the woman to accept my role or to continue rejecting that I was the only nurse assigned to her husband at that moment. I simply left the room before the woman could say anything else. Unfortunately, I have run into many people that still believed we lived in the 1920s. Skin tone does not make a person competent or incompetent, but there were other cases where patients or their family members assumed I was the janitor or maintenance person and not the nurse simply because of my skin.

Since I had a job, I also had good medical insurance. This allowed my family and me to obtain quality medical care. When I began having heavy bleeding and pain, I was able to go to the doctor. I was diagnosed with fibroids.

Today, women have many alternatives to try when dealing with fibroids before a hysterectomy is required. Sadly, these were not available or only in experimental stages at that time. Instead, it was common practice to perform a hysterectomy on women suffering from this ailment, something that is seen as a last resort today since it is considered a major surgery.

Taking time off from anything was hard for me, especially since I loved my work.

In my case, when they performed the surgery, my ovaries were also removed. This meant that my body was suddenly not receiving all the natural hormones it needed to regulate it. I was thrown into early menopause. With regular menopause, women slowly stop producing estrogen. This gradual decrease affects women in different ways, but the change is usually slow enough that women can pass through this stage in their lives without additional medication or treatment.

When surgical procedures such as the one I had cause menopause, the drop in estrogen is drastic. The resulting symptoms are severe. Hot flashes that are uncomfortable to women in natural menopause become unbearable to women who experience surgery-induced menopause. Severe menopause after surgery causes sleep problems, chills, incontinence, night sweats, thinning hair, increased bladder infections, weight gain, moodiness, headaches, and dry skin. In my case, it also made me nauseous and caused me to have heart palpitations. After seeing my doctor for these side effects, he decided the problems were related to being on my feet all day long and told me I needed to take some time off from work.

I had pushed myself my whole life. Taking time off from anything was hard for me, especially since I loved my work. Although some of my patients looked at me through eyes of prejudice, the staff at the hospital was great, and I enjoyed being a part of the team. Still, I did not want to die an early death because of my stubborn desire to keep working, so I took the time off. This gave me time to spend focusing more on my family.

My oldest son did surprisingly well in the Marines. He graduated from basic training and then went on to train at Camp Lejeune in Jacksonville, North Carolina. I visited him when he graduated and was pleasantly surprised to find an entirely different young man. The Marines turned him from a belligerent, angry youth into a well-mannered gentleman. When he finished all his training, he shipped off to Hawaii.

Chapter 13

After I recovered, I ended up working at several hospitals in Florida. Sometimes I had to change hospitals to reduce the distance I drove to work. In other cases, poor leadership motivated my desire to find new employment. At one hospital, I was the charge nurse on the critical care unit. While I was there, they wanted to build a cardiac intervention unit. Since I had experience in this area, they had another nurse and I work together to design it. We were able to give our input about how to set up the beds and equipment. We also had to come up with the protocols for the new unit. I was completely in my element. All of this movement was a step in the direction God was taking me.

There were other times when things at the hospital did not go well. As the charge nurse, I had to make rounds and check the patients. One patient was doing poorly after surgery. Her blood pressure kept dropping, which is never a good sign.

I immediately called the doctor. This doctor was not the patient's doctor, who had performed the initial surgery, but instead, it was the doctor covering for the patient's doctor. When I told the on-call doctor what I saw and that the patient's blood pressure kept dropping, he did not seem concerned. The on-call doctor stated he would come to the hospital and examine the patient himself.

As I hung up the phone, I was visibly upset. I would not sit back and allow this patient to die without doing all that I could for her. Since I was the charge nurse, I was allowed to make some administrative decisions. We had standing protocols for complications so I went ahead and wrote a verbal order for the ultrasound which was the only test that could prove if there was a bleed or not. However, once I finished ordering the test, there was little else I could do until the doctor arrived. I waited as the ultrasound was performed, but the doctor had still not arrived at the hospital. The only other thing I could do to help the woman before the doctor arrived was pray.

Finally, the on-call doctor arrived. He called the surgeon and took the poor woman to surgery to stop the bleeding. Unfortunately, she died on the operating table.

After the frustrating experience of trying to get the woman help, I was ready to quit working at that hospital. I cared about people, or I would not have become a nurse. I did my best to improve my knowledge so that I could be an asset to the doctors. I did not want to work where money was valued above life, nor did I want to work where the nurse was not a trusted member of the medical team. The other nurses convinced me that I could make a difference by being a patient advocate, so I continued working at that hospital a while longer. Sadly, the hospital continued to make financial decisions over the quality of care.

Soon, we got a new supervisor. Probably the worst change the supervisor made was with the scheduling. The previous supervisor had us on a set schedule. This new supervisor's motto of "change for change's sake" showed in the rotating schedule that was established. Every week, the nurses would be on a different schedule. Days this week, nights the next, and a mixed schedule the following. There was no way to determine when you were going to work until after you saw the schedule. It was impossible to plan doctor's appointments or even a trip to watch my son's football games because I never knew when I was going to be working. Since sleep schedules were constantly changed, we all had to operate under conditions of sleep deprivation, which made us less alert. After many complaints, a ward that operated in a disorganized manner, and many more prayers, we finally got a better supervisor.

Time was passing. I began working part-time and teaching in a practical nursing program full-time. I was able to teach in the practical nursing program while I pursued my master's degree in nursing. My role as a nurse changed, but now I was helping other young people to join me in my career. Although doctors were sometimes arrogant, once I was a licensed nurse, I did not have many problems with discrimination from the hospital staff. I did continue to have patients that would ask me to see the nurse, assuming that my rank was not on my badge but on my skin. This was difficult to work through emotionally, but I did my best to keep a smile on my face. Few were as resistant as the lady who refused to believe me or her husband.

Although I put a lot into nursing, that did not keep Robert and me from being active members of our church. I worked with the youth, the women's ministry retreat, and I was the Sabbath School superintendent. Even in this, there came some strife. At the church, a woman named Betty began complaining about how well I was doing the job of Sabbath School superintendent. Since I had already been through all the strife in New York when I was elected to be church clerk, I decided I would not go through it again. I simply told the woman I would be happy to step down, and she could take over for me.

Christians should always look for ways to serve Him and do His work. "As each one has received a gift, minister it to one another, as good stewards of the manifold grace of God" (1 Peter 4:10). God has given each of us our abilities and talents. It is our privilege to use them in ways that glorify Him. If a door to one ministry closes, it does not give us an excuse to stop doing the Lord's work. Sometimes you might have to make your own ministry if a formal one does not exist at your church.

As a nurse, I made it my job to seek out the sick and elderly in the church and minister to them. In some cases, their bodies were riddled with cancer. Jack was one of those cases. He had liver cancer and was in the hospital. I would go visit him and his family there and give them encouragement. As a nurse, I could touch their lives on a whole new level. I would not only pray for them but also act as a sort of medical interpreter to help explain some of the confusing medical terminologies to the patients as well as their families. A better understanding of the conditions and treatments relieved some of the stress they felt during those difficult times.

In 2001, all the nursing faculty from the school were standing around in the break room when we saw the plane crash into New York's Twin Towers on television. Everyone watched in amazement. We could not believe what we were seeing on television. Then the second plane hit. When we finished watching the tragedy of 9/11 unfold, someone went over and shut off the television. We were too upset to continue teaching. We canceled classes, and everyone went home.

Chapter 14

The events of 9/11 caused me to reexamine my own life. When I came to the United States in 1986, I had nothing. I arrived without a job, without a place to stay, and without my children. I wasn't married, and I didn't even have a high school diploma. Now, I had my family, a steady job, a house, an education, and anything I needed. I could not have expected how drastically my life would change when I arrived here. I was only hoping for something better than what I had in Jamaica. If I had stayed on that island, I would have never been able to become a nurse. I might not have even found my way back to God. After much reflection, I decided it was time for me to repay my new country. I went down and applied to join the Army. I was forty-five years old.

I was initially proud of my decision to serve my country. When I started talking to other people about it, however, they told me horror stories. I started having second thoughts. The days ticked past, and I began to wonder if my application would even be accepted since I had to apply with a waiver because of my age. I prayed seriously and asked God to have my application denied if He could.

Then, I got the phone call to come in for an interview. I was nervous, but I went in and passed it. I began to get anxious again. I kept praying about the situation. Next, I got a call from the recruiter. I told him I was not sure if I still wanted to go, but he told me that all my paperwork had made it up to Colonel Gordon at the Nursing Corps. When I hung up the phone, I began to cry. I prayed for the Lord to somehow get me out of this new situation. Suddenly, I felt peace. Instead of the answer I was expecting, the Holy Spirit told me to go. When Colonel Gordon called me, I was sobbing, and through the tears, I told her I really did not want to go, but the Holy Spirit had directed me to go.

Because of my experience and education, I joined as an officer. I had not done much exercise, so my husband started exercising with me each day. I knew basic training was going to be both physically and mentally challenging. I signed my Oath of Office on September 16, 2002. My oldest son got a leave of absence to come home and watch me sign it. There were also a few friends from the church and my husband to witness the event. They shipped me off to basic training after I signed my oath.

Officer basic training was a whole new experience. In addition to all the exercise, we also did long hikes and camping. I even rappelled for the first time down the makeshift obstacle course even though I was afraid of heights. Sadly, after I joined the military, my husband and I began having trouble with my youngest son. Before this time, he was an easygoing kid who got good grades and played football. Now, he changed. Whether it was hitting the troubled teen years (he was twelve) or whether it was because I had to be gone from the home for much longer periods of time, it is unclear. Whatever the reason, he became rebellious.

Although I was still a nurse in the military, it was a different atmosphere. In the civilian world, I felt like I had more independence in making some decisions for my patients. The military seemed to function more as a unit, which means that everyone is dependent on each other. Unlike the civilian hospitals, I think the military rules were there to promote efficiency. Instead of, "Wait—okay, hurry up!" as it was in the civilian world, the military was "Hurry up—okay, wait!" This attitude allowed me to do all I could and then wait for the next authorization. To me, this preparedness made much more sense.

The problem was that I had gotten used to simply doing what I could by myself. In the military, I would still try to make independent decisions, but these got me in more minor troubles than I could count. There was a lot I could do, but when I stepped out of those bounds and did something without the authorization, I was reprimanded.

The Lord has promised if you follow Him and "make the Most High your dwelling, no harm will overtake you, no disaster will come near your tent" (Ps. 91:9b–10, NIV). I joined the military in response to a call from the Holy Spirit to do so. Throughout all my adjustment period, the Lord was with me, guiding and protecting me. Only the Lord can take care of you no matter where you are or what you are doing. Only He can give you peace and protection from this world.

Once I finished my training and was taught how to be a nurse in the military, my first duty station was at Fort Stewart in Georgia. After being away from my family for weeks, we were now back together again. The Lord had taken me away, but He safely brought me back and would continue to do this.

At Fort Stewart, I worked in the ICU (Intensive Care Unit) as the charge nurse. Although there is a set order for the military, when the military employs civilians, the civilians do not have to follow some of the military rules. An active military nurse, like myself, would only be stationed at the hospital for about two years before receiving orders to move on to the next station. The civilian nurses had worked there much longer than that, and they knew if they did not like someone that they only had to wait them out until they were transferred.

I did not stay long at Fort Stewart. In 2005, I got my orders to deploy to Iraq. When I joined the military, my friends had all warned me of the dangers of working in a war zone, even as a nurse. At Fort Stewart, I knew I would eventually be called to deployment, but there were bases all over the United States and even in Europe that provided support to our frontline troops. I was scared to go to a place that was so unfamiliar—a place where the next day might be my last.

Again, I got down on my knees and began diligently praying. "Please, Lord, I don't want to go there. Please, let me stay home." The Holy Spirit answered this prayer quickly. I was guided to stop praying and start packing because I had to go to Iraq.

"Please, Lord, I don't want to go there. Please, let me stay home."

Part of my dislike for heading into a war-torn country across the sea came from my dislike of flying. When you are stateside, the military can fly you somewhere, or you can take a bus to your next destination. Not so when that destination is halfway around the world. When my plane left from Fort Campbell in Kentucky, I spent more than nineteen hours on the plane. The Lord had mercy on me, and my flight to Kuwait was uneventful.

I remember stepping off that plane and standing there for a moment in shock. Kuwait was covered in snow! My images of Kuwait were always filled with sand. To see snow on top of everything surprised me.

However, Kuwait was not to be our final post. We stayed there for Christmas, though, so we tried our best to cheer up the soldiers who had been stationed there for a while. Soon enough, we were transferred to our final destination.

By the time we arrived in southern Iraq, the standardized modular field hospital was already set up, but the place where we were to live was not. The average temperature in January was about fifty-five degrees Fahrenheit, so there was no snow on the ground, but it was not a sunny, warm place either. We were there to replace another unit, but that unit had not yet moved out of the trailers. As a result, we needed to stay in tents until that transition could take place.

Tents

Although there was no snow in that area of Iraq, January happens to be the month where they get the largest amount of rainfall. This was more weather I was not expecting. So far, my first experiences with the desert weather had been snow and rain. The rain was so hard that my tent caved in from the weight of the rainfall. Since the desert ground does not absorb rain well, we ended up with many "lakes" and muddy areas. All of us were thankful when we could finally move into the more stable trailer housing.

The base did not have different Christian denominational meetings. We had one chaplain, and all of us attended one service. There was also a weekly Bible study offered that I gladly attended. It was at church that I ran into my unit's chief nurse, and it was there that I discovered she was also a Seventh-day Adventist.

One night, as I was sleeping in one of the trailers, I woke up to the sound of what I thought was an earthquake or a tornado, or perhaps both at once. The ground was not moving, and so I thought we were being attacked. I hurried to put on my flak vest and my helmet. I had no idea what new act of war was approaching, but it was extremely loud. Once I was suited up, I curled up in my bed with the sound growing outside and began to pray. I heard a small voice in the midst of it telling me to read Psalm 91, which I did. The noise did not stop. Finally, I could stand it no longer and crept to the door and opened it a crack to peer out.

When I realized what it was, I instantly closed the door. In that small instant, the giant sandstorm had not only plastered my face and clothing with sand but also had coated the inside of my room in it. I stood there with eyes that were tearing after being blasted with sand. The wind was roaring, and it was pitch black outside, but I had no idea what to do. I knew that I did not need to be wearing my gear. Not only was this act of nature not the act of war I initially imagined but I also knew that no military actions could be performed during it.

As I pulled off my vest, sand fell from it. Everything I had on was coated in it. When the large grains fell off, they left behind a fine dust. I went back to my bed only to find it was also coated in sand. I cleaned it off and decided there was nothing I could do except go back to sleep. As I lay on the bed, I had to cover my ears to block out the roaring wind. In the morning, I woke up to the mess that had invaded my home. I finished cleaning my trailer, happy I only had to survive a sandstorm through the night instead of a bombing firestorm.

Chapter 15

During my deployment to Iraq, the doctor went out the gate of the compound each morning, and Iraqi civilians would crowd around the entrance with their sick and wounded, hoping to get medical care. The doctor had to examine each case and had to determine who needed our services the most because of our limited resources. There were always so many children among the wounded, and there was also a high percentage of people with burns—adults and children alike.

Since we were designed to only treat adults when the hospital was created, this meant we needed to find an area in the hospital to dedicate to treating children when we were able to begin treating them. Since I had worked in the PICU when I was still in Florida, I was assigned to many of the children who came through the hospital doors for treatment. I often would use my own money to purchase the children items online as I cared for them.

I remember one particular case when a three-year-old little girl was admitted to the hospital. She was so thin and frail that she looked as if she were only about six months old. Her parents brought her to us because she had not been eating, and so she kept losing weight. She was diagnosed with an intestinal problem. She needed surgery to correct it, but we only had tools to do surgery for an adult. In addition, the military medical training we received only focused on adults. Although we were taught how to improvise and scale some things down, this girl was so tiny she was the size of an infant. She was so small we sewed together some bandages for a makeshift blanket.

She made it through the surgery, but we were uncertain if she would survive. We all were very gentle when caring for her. She was so small, and we did not want to hurt her. Her size made it extremely stressful and scary to treat her. Throughout her entire recovery from the surgery, we were worried we would lose her. Slowly, as she recovered, she began to gain some weight. We all celebrated the day she went home with her family.

A while later, the family brought her back, worried something new was wrong with her. We brought her in to examine her again. None of us wanted to lose this tiny girl who we had worked so hard to keep alive. After the examination, we were relieved to discover that she was just getting fatter from being able to eat. The family did not realize how quickly a healthy child grows.

Near to the military base was the famed Ziggurat of Ur. The Bible tells us in Genesis 11:31, "And Terah took his son Abram and his grandson Lot, the son of Haran, and his daughter-in-law Sarai, his son Abram's wife, and they went out with them from Ur of the Chaldeans to go to the land of Canaan." The Ziggurat of Ur or Great Ziggurat and the area around it was excavated by Sir Leonard Woolley in the 1920s. What he found rivaled the discovery of King Tutankhamen's tomb. The same city of Ur mentioned in the Bible is the city that surrounded the Ziggurat.

Zigguraut

I was able to go to Ur and walk where Abraham walked. The Ziggurat itself was a temple devoted to the goddess Nanna in ancient times. Much work went into restoring it in the 1980s, especially since the structure was originally made of unbaked mud brick on the inside and baked mud brick on the outside of it. It was difficult work, and only the bottom two levels have been restored. Unlike the Egyptian pyramids, the ziggurat is stepped, and there are no passages inside. However, the tomb of Ur-Nammu, an ancient king who might have been ruling when Abraham lived in Ur, is still visible at the site. The Iraqi people are very proud of their ancient cities in the same way Americans are proud of the White House and some of our architectural achievements. Sadly, the site at Ur was deteriorating when I was there because the Iraqi government did not have enough money to preserve it any longer.

We were allowed to visit some of the tombs and carved-out places. Similar to other pagan cultures, when a royal died, the additional bodies in that person's tomb were servants sacrificed to supposedly help the dead person in the afterlife. Sir Woolley found more than 1,800 bodies in the tombs, and many of those were the result of being sacrificed upon the death of a member of the royalty. In one case, a single tomb contained more than seventy bodies.

After seeing the tombs, we were taken to the supposed home of Abraham. Whether this home was truly his or not, I don't think anyone can determine. Wherever Abraham lived, the idolatrous temple and the tombs where people were sacrificed surrounded him. It is no wonder that God called the patriarch out of this land. In Canaan, as a shepherd, he was able to begin a new life devoted to God without distractions.

Ur died as a city because the river that ran alongside it shifted, and the life it brought to the desert died as the water moved away. Perhaps God knew that Ur was not a place where He could raise His people to follow Him. Perhaps God had a hand in turning the river away from the pagan society. For whatever reason, God called Abraham out of Ur and allowed that civilization to die. God is our Living Water. We need to build our homes near Him so that we do not become dry and desolate like the desert.

As I thought about how God had called Abraham away from his home—a thriving city—into a land that was less civilized, I thought about how that allowed Abraham to focus more on God. Then I thought about my own life. I had been in the middle of a successful nursing career in the United States, but I still had many issues from my past that I had not yet overcome. Perhaps this was a place in the wilderness where I would be able to confront those issues so I could focus on God.

Chapter 16

I have no idea why so many who came to us had been burned, but caring for burn patients, especially children, was traumatic for me. War began to take its toll, and I was not even on the frontlines putting my own life at risk every day. One day, a girl came in horribly burned. We performed CPR, but she still died. I walked away from her bed with tears in my eyes.

"I can't deal with this!" I shouted. Everyone was staring at me. My superior took me aside and told me that I was not behaving appropriately as an officer or as a nurse. I was devastated. I knew she was right. What kind of hope was I giving my patients if I let them know that I felt there was nothing that could be done to help them?

Another woman already had an IV in her arm when I began caring for her. It is important to begin rehydrating burn patients as soon as possible. Surprisingly, once the burning is stopped, hypothermia can occur if the patient is not carefully wrapped in bandages to prevent heat loss. Burned skin no longer has the ability to insulate the body. The bad thing is that burn patients are also prone to infection, so the bandages must be changed at least once a day. Since the gauze sticks to the wound, the only way to change this woman's bandages was by sedating her. Every time we tried to carefully pull a bandage off, her skin would come off with it. Even when we were not changing her bandages, she was in constant, agonizing pain. To make matters more traumatizing for me, she was the mother of a two- or three-month-old baby. The woman grew progressively worse until machines were the only thing still keeping her alive.

At that point, we had to explain her situation to her family. We let them know that if we shut off the machines, she would die. Understandably, the family did not want this at first, but after several days they returned and told us to shut off the machines. When the woman passed away, her entire family began to wail. I knew that these could be dangerous people who harbored a hatred of America in general, and by extension, they would also hate me. We were trained to keep a cautious distance, but I could not resist giving each family member a hug and reaching out to a fellow human who was in a state of mourning.

I had to work with so many burn patients in Iraq that I vowed I would never take care of another burn patient again. There were many horrors of war—unspeakable things—that were not meant for any human eye to see or heart to bear, but the burn patients struck me the deepest. Every day tore my conscience. I knew I was doing what was medically necessary by changing the old bandages, but I was also causing someone severe physical pain as I inadvertently ripped their skin off with the gauze. It was so bad that I even remember when one person's ear fell off in my hand as I was trying to delicately remove the old dressings.

The call to step away from my past was a struggle. I carried my abuse with me every day.

There was no escape from the new trauma I was exposed to each day. I could not even immerse myself in the church or volunteer activities after my shift because there was little to do on the base. I did enjoy the Bible study as a break from my duties, but it was one of few things that distracted me from the pain and suffering in the hospital. Soon after my arrival, the Bible study began working through *The Purpose-Driven Life* by Rick Warren.

As I went through this book and studied it in a multi-denominational setting, I learned more about myself. The main point of the devotional seems to be that we need to put our past behind us and focus on serving God. This is a goal many Christians can agree on despite their denominational background, and so it was very popular across different branches of Christianity.

For me, the call to step away from my past was a struggle. I carried my abuse with me every day. I questioned why my past had happened to me. Where was God when I needed protection from those who were supposed to protect me? I began a vigil of praying. One night, as I prayed, I felt a deep well of emotions that traveled from my gut up to my throat, and I started crying in almost an animalistic way. The sobbing went on for quite a while until I fell asleep. I awoke the next day feeling as if a load was off my head. It felt as if my entire past was lifted from me. As I sat on the steps of my trailer, I asked God why did He let me suffer all those years.

Then a brightness came over me, and I heard a voice that told me I was there in Iraq because the Lord had to get me by myself so He could give me the victory and deliver me. Just as He had pulled Abraham away to the wilderness, He had pulled me to Iraq.

The Lord's voice comforted me. Yes, a step-by-step plan to rid yourself of all troubles in forty days might be what everyone wants to hear, but the biblical fact is that God continues working on you for the rest of your life once you make a commitment to Him. The revelation that God was with me and helping me was a relief.

In Iraq, I maintained my faith and Adventist diet, but the spiritual education I was getting was sometimes subtly contradicting what I knew. God had called me away from home to work on myself—He made that very clear. However the conflicting emotions and struggles over my past converged with the stresses of treating the burn victims in ways that helped them but subjected them to enormous pain. Under all this stress, there was no question of if I was going to break. The question was when it would happen.

Chapter 17

It appears as if many women and children are not valued in various cultures, and in Iraq, this was very evident. The men were always the first to come to the gates of the compound. They were assessed like everyone else, but the women and children were usually more critical. In addition, the children we saw seemed to be always hungry because it appeared as if the family dynamics had an hierarchy of male first and everyone else secondary. For this reason, when children were admitted to our hospital, we would prepare the child's tray with all his or her nutritional needs on it, and then we would prepare a separate tray for the family to prevent them from taking the recovering child's food.

I somewhat understand the logic behind this mentality. The man does the work and brings the food home. The child does not. The man needs more food to continue working. The child does not. However, I, personally, had gone without food so my own children could eat. Many people have logical reasons for doing what they do. In my book, children are the next generation. They need so much more to thrive and grow properly.

In one case at the hospital, this issue of who gets to eat first was even more pronounced. We were struggling to help a boy gain weight so he could undergo further procedures. We would prepare the trays for the family and separate trays for the boy, but when we would go back into the room, everything was gone. We could not understand why the boy was still not gaining weight. One day, we caught the boy's mother. She first slipped her food into her purse and then took the boy's food and did the same. Apparently, she was taking her food and her child's food home so the other members of her family would have a meal. Experiences like these reinforced the need for Americans and others to be appreciative of what we have and use these blessings to bless others. To whom much is given, much is required.

To resolve this food issue, we never dropped the trays off inside the room and left again. A nurse would go into the room with the trays and stay there while the boy ate. Our presence was enough to discourage the mother from taking any more food home with her. Not surprisingly, the boy finally began to gain weight. Once he weighed enough, we were able to airlift him to another hospital so he could have surgery.

On the other hand, one thinks that children are always innocent, but in times of war, you never know whom you can trust. One little nomadic boy came into the hospital with his body filled with shrapnel. He had been out in a mine-filled field looking for some water for his family. He placed his foot on the wrong spot, and a mine exploded. I knew he had undergone much pain, which probably made him so hateful toward Americans. As I was giving him his medications, he lifted his thumb skyward and pointed two fingers at me in the shape of a gun. He proceeded to act as if he was shooting me. Although the hospital took numerous precautions to prevent members of the opposition from entering our hospital under the false pretenses of someone who is injured and in need of help, there was never any certainty about whether or not that person you were trying to help would turn on you.

The base was located on a plain that made direct attacks unlikely, but there was the constant threat of a missile or bombing attack. When we went on alert, there were many times we would huddle together in the trailers and pray. The Lord always protected us. The bombs never directly hit. When our unit finally went home, only one person in it had ever been shot, and all of us made it back home alive.

Once, I was tired and in desperate need of a shower. Every time I got my shower stuff ready and headed to the shower, the alarm would sound at the most inopportune time. I could not take the shower in the middle of an alert, so I went into action and prepared for the attack. When the danger passed, I could no longer take a shower because I had other duties. The next time I had a free moment, I got my stuff ready for a shower again. Once again, the alarm went off. All week long, I tried to take a shower and could not.

Another time, I was working the night shift at the military hospital. That meant I needed to sleep during the day, which is always difficult under the best of conditions. Tiredness and loss of empathy are two obvious signs of sleep deprivation. To make matters worse, one soldier would play some of the foulest music I ever heard during the day. It is impossible to get any sleep when someone is playing loud, awful music. Since the soldier was angry at me, I knew she was doing this on purpose. Asking her to turn it down would not stop her from doing it the next day.

There were so many stressors on me: working nights, dealing with children and their parents who did not put them first, living in constant fear that a missile would hit the base from afar. It was all too much. One day, I could bear it no longer. My military training was supposed to be there to help me perform tasks automatically by instinct under the worst of situations, and that is what I did.

I had just fallen asleep when that horrible music blared through my dreams to wake me up yet again. I did not think. I reacted. I got up from my bed, grabbed my 9mm pistol, and walked over to the woman playing it. I told her I was going to blow her head off if she didn't shut the music off immediately.

Needless to say, I was referred to the chaplain for my actions. After talking to me about my feelings in that moment and the other feelings I had toward the soldier, he recommended I go in for a psychological evaluation. There I was diagnosed with depression and Post-Traumatic Stress Disorder (PTSD). I was removed from the night shift to help ease some of my stress and allow me some much-needed sleep.

I was also assigned as in addition to working the emergency room as well as the ICU a Medevac nurse. Medevac is when you transfer one patient to another hospital in a helicopter or airplane. I was required to help load the patients onto the airplane and make sure they were stable during the flight. I was terrified of flying, but I knew that this was just another challenge I must overcome. Sometimes these flights went to a hospital in Germany, but other times they went all the way to the United States. These soldiers were the ones we could not treat, and many were in critical condition. I was finally getting more sleep at night, but my days were filled with living nightmares. Looking back at these experiences and others about which I would never speak, I know God held me in the palm of His hand.

At the same time as my transfer to days, I began treatment for my PTSD and the depression and anger issues that resulted from it. I also started attending a prayer and support group that allowed me to not only receive support but also to offer my support to those around me. This put me in a position to help others navigate the nuances of military life. In some cases, I was able to pass problems some of the other members had up the chain of command to help ease some of these soldiers' troubles.

For example, one soldier was in a bad marriage. Her husband would leave their kids at home or force her mother to take care of them. Since she did not initially think he would take advantage of her, she naturally had a joint bank account with him. The military deposited all her paychecks in it. However, he was not a good husband, so he would simply withdraw all the money and spend it on frivolities. I did everything I could to help her to get leave so she could go home and set up a new bank account. She had to go through the paperwork of having the checks deposited in the new account, but at least her husband was no longer able to steal her hard-earned money from her.

God has commanded us in Proverbs 3:27, "Do not withhold good from those to whom it is due, When it is in the power of your hand to do so." Sometimes the easier choice is to ignore what good we can do. We might be too tired, too stressed out, afraid that our efforts will not work or be enough, or we might think there are plenty of other people around to do the job who could do it better than us. We must realize that God is faithful. He will give us the strength to do what needs to be done as long as we take the initiative to do it. We also have to understand that God's plans do not always conclude with us. We might not be able to get the person to the endpoint that is best for them, but we can help them navigate the steps along the way or provide them support to reassure them that others care about them.

Chapter 18

On November 21, 2006, I returned home. I had completed my master's degree while I was stationed in Iraq through a distance-learning program. At that time, the next step in my career was to become a nurse practitioner. I wanted to move on and start a new part of my life. After applying, I was accepted to the Army's nurse practitioner program. I was able to unwind a little when I returned to Fort Stewart in Georgia before I needed to move to Maryland and begin the program.

The Uniformed Services University of the Health Sciences in Maryland is a graduate school solely for military personnel. In order to be accepted, you must be an officer in the Army, Navy, Air Force, or U.S. Public Health Service. The education is free, but you must commit to another seven years of active-duty service if you attend.

Committing was not a problem for me. I loved the military and already planned to spend the rest of my life in it. I was optimistic as my family prepared for the move. I was also glad that my hard work allowed me to be accepted into the university since it was such a competitive program. Only about nine percent of all applicants make it. Here is another place God worked His will in my life.

Since the family nurse practitioner was more advanced than a regular nursing program, one of my classes was a lab where we dissected human cadavers. After all my time treating people who were alive and in pain, you would think that dissecting a human cadaver would have been easy. Unfortunately, it was not. Every day, I would finish the required work, and then I would take a break to go outside and cry. I wanted to be a nurse practitioner so badly, but I could not understand why I was having such a hard time getting through this basic course.

At the time, I did not realize PTSD could affect my life in so many ways. I believed that my fear, and not my PTSD, was crippling my life. I thought that if I only loved God more, I would be able to push myself through this traumatic experience. The problem is that the fear PTSD causes is not logical. It takes something that you do every single day and turns it against you.

So, I continued my torturous routine. I would work on the cadaver and weep outside afterward. I knew something was wrong, but I thought that something was me and not the bad way my body was reacting to the trauma of war. Then, one day, I was told to begin working on a tall, male cadaver.

As I stared at the body, I noticed his dark skin. This man had the darkest skin I had ever seen in my life. At that moment, he was no longer just a cadaver. He became a real person to me—he put a face on death. I had taken care of so many open-heart surgery patients before the war and was so amazed by the wonder of the human heart. There was no reason for this man to have caused me any problems, but as I began to examine his arteries, I could no longer handle it. I ran out of the room, screaming uncontrollably. Needless to say, my outburst was not unnoticed.

I was sent to Walter Reed Army Medical Center (now the Walter Reed National Military Medical Center) for inpatient/outpatient treatment of my PTSD. I had to be there from 8:00 a.m. until 5:00 p.m. every day. There are several treatments and medications for people with PTSD. One doctor treating me wanted me to begin writing out all the events that had happened so that I could revisit them in a safe environment. After I was finished with my treatment I was reassigned to a teaching position. I was no longer assigned to work on the floor to help further remove me from additional trauma. Instead, I worked with the chief nurse and was later assigned as a nursing faculty in the nursing program.

My breakdown resulted in me being unable to complete my degree at the Uniformed Services University of the Health Sciences. I was still driven to finish my education and make it to the next level. I applied to Duke and was accepted into their distance-learning program. In the two-and-a-half years that I worked educating other nurses, I was able to finish my courses for the nurse practitioner at Duke. However, I did not take the required exams to qualify me to work as a nurse practitioner. I made this decision for personal reasons, and I never felt called to work in that area. The knowledge I gained had been enough to allow me to be the best nurse I could be.

Throughout my struggle with PTSD, I was constantly trying to assess myself and see if I was fulfilling my purpose. I now know that it is not about overcoming my fears of abuse or anger to find my purpose. My purpose is simple: I was made to bring glory to God in all that I do. I work for Him. My real struggle at the time was actually to find out what purpose there was in everything bad that had happened to me.

The problem is that we do not (or should not) sign up to be a Christian simply because we want a trouble-free life. We should sign up to be a Christian because we love the Lord, and we want to serve Him because He sent His Son to die for us. Job loved God and had bad times. Jeremiah loved God and had bad times. The apostles loved God and had bad times. We suffer bad times because we live in a fallen world. Even Jesus, our Perfect Example, fulfilled His purpose but went through suffering along the way.

I realized that I had been abused because I live in a fallen world. I had to go through the abuse of my youth and go to Iraq and witness all those horrors of war because I lived in a fallen world. Although that process was painful, it allowed me to see that God will not abandon me no matter where I am or what is happening around me. If I turn to Him and His Word, He will help me sleep in His arms even through the worst sandstorm. The bad part of this is that sometimes you are not able to share your witness because you are being judged and looked down upon by others.

When the trauma of war was in the distant past, I was transferred to Tripler Army Medical Center in Honolulu, Hawaii. I had achieved the rank of major and became the head nurse of the cardiovascular department. After about a year I was promoted to nurse director of the large Family Medicine Clinic.

The medical director of that clinic at the time I was there was also a Christian. We would often collaborate on the best policies to implement, and then both of us would mention it during meetings or to the appropriate persons. One project we worked to implement concerned making the facility an accredited patient-centered medical home. This is one of the highest standards in health care that recognizes when a hospital ensures its patients receive the highest quality of care. It is meant to distinguish hospitals that go above and beyond nationally recognized standards. We were successful in our project.

While I was in Hawaii, one of my sons had a terrible motorcycle accident in Germany. He was at a birthday party and decided to go on a ride with several friends. This was a choice that would change his life. When I was first contacted, I learned very little about how the accident happened, but I did know the extent of his injuries and how serious they were.

When I arrived in Germany and saw the MRI, I realized my son's leg was completely splintered, and I was afraid he was going to lose it. I called every prayer warrior, even in the churches I had previously attended in other states, and requested prayer. He had fractured his sternum, broken his arm, and basically destroyed one leg.

My son told me when the bike skidded, and he flew up in the air, he heard a voice telling him he would be okay—He would not let him die. My son said a peace came over him between hearing that voice and hitting the ground. Today, with the exception of intermittent pain and occasional limps, he is okay. He has since given his life to Christ and, like most of us, is living his life under grace and seeking God day by day. After helping my son through this time, I returned to my station in Hawaii.

One of the best things about living in Hawaii was that I could get many of the fruits and vegetables I had loved in Jamaica. In Hawaii, they were freshly grown. They had many farmers' markets, and the other towns on Oahu were all within easy driving reach (except during rush hour), making it easy to go looking elsewhere if I couldn't find exactly what I was looking for at one of them. However, as with any place on earth, the good comes with the bad.

he heard a voice telling him he would be okay— He would not let him die.

Although I grew up on an island, Jamaica is among the biggest islands in the Caribbean. Oahu, where I was stationed, was more than seven times smaller than my country of birth.

Not surprisingly, most people who move to Oahu leave within a year. In part, this is because traditional job opportunities are limited to the hospitality industry and medical occupations, and Hawaii can be one of the most expensive places to live in the United States. Even prices at the commissary seemed higher than in other places I had lived.

Another big part of the reason people leave Hawaii is "island fever." When you live in a place where you can drive from one coast to the other in an hour and a half, you begin to realize how limited the space is. The ocean seems as if it is a vast pit, preventing you from seeing the rest of the world. The people who survive the confinement are usually those who never get bored of relaxing activities like walking on the beach. Hawaii is a great vacation spot, but it takes a special kind of non-native person to live there permanently. I am one of those special people. I would return there to live if I could.

I was an active duty military nurse, so although I had to deal with high prices, I also had a steady income and job security. These things, along with my island upbringing, allowed me to feel comfortable in this setting.

Because of the constant inflow and outflow of "residents," island natives, who are some of the sweetest, friendliest people you could meet sometimes, tend to be standoffish to new residents. After all, who wants to build a friendship when that person will only be there a short time before you will have to go through the emotional heartbreak of losing another friend? Because of this, non-native residents tend to find it difficult to quickly develop emotional support on the island. In the public schools, this can be especially tough on children. Parents who call home to ask for advice might also be met with a lot of "but you live in Hawaii." Thankfully, my youngest son had already finished high school, and by being in the military, I was already surrounded by a support system.

Although I have some good memories of Hawaii and would return there any day, my next assignment was a move to Fort Hood in Texas. Fort Hood is where my oldest son and his family were also assigned, so I looked forward to this transfer for those reasons.

Chapter 19

I had entered the military at an older age than most people. After more than a decade of active duty, my age began to affect my health. I still struggled with PTSD, which was not age-related. In addition, I was prone to shin splints and hearing problems. As I was approaching sixty, I developed diabetes.

Diabetes is a disease that occurs when your body is not managing sugar properly. Type II diabetes (sometimes called adult-onset diabetes) happens when you do not make enough insulin to move the sugars throughout your body systems. It is also possible your body just stops responding to the insulin you do make. Blurred vision, fatigue, weight loss, and frequent infections are some of the symptoms, but many times you can have diabetes silently affecting your health for a while before you realize it.

The problems for diabetics in the military occur when they require insulin to maintain their health. Insulin requires refrigeration for storage, and there are many places in the field where it would be difficult for soldiers to receive or maintain access to any medications. Although the likelihood of my being in a place without refrigeration was low, the military has set rules that cover everyone.

My medical provider at the time was also a Seventh-day Adventist. She knew the benefits of a healthy lifestyle and a biblical diet. We both knew that unless I could get my sugar levels under control, she was required to refer me to the Medical Evaluation Board. Before she sent the recommendation to the Medical Evaluation Board, she allowed me to make changes to my routine through exercise and diet in an attempt to control my diabetes without medication.

In my case, I could not get my blood sugar levels under control. Instead of my efforts lowering them, they increased. After more than fifteen years in the military, I was medically retired. I enjoyed the military so much. I did not want to leave. I was working on my doctorate because I wanted to secure an assignment in the nursing research department. But God's plans for me did not include a longer stay in the military.

When the Med Board told me my military career was finished, I protested. I told them I would appeal their decision because I had big plans to further my career in the military after completing my doctoral degree.

I was also dealing with degenerative disk disease. Depending on your range of motion, this will not disqualify you from active military duty, but it does cause immense pain. I was upset that my body was telling me to retire before I was willing to do it.

I spoke with my provider about options I might have to continue my military service. She was sympathetic but told me to look at it as a blessing in disguise. I could never have imagined the road ahead of me, but God knew what was about to happen, and my retirement was a blessing in disguise.

Maj Nicholls

Just before my final out-processing, my husband had a cerebellar stroke. In these, the blood supply is interrupted in the section of the brain that is at the back of your head on top of your spine. This part of the brain is directly in charge of balance and movement. In order to treat this kind of stroke, the doctors needed to get rid of the blood clot that formed, and then the patient, in this case, my husband, has to undergo therapy to regain the abilities that were lost.

I had to use some of my leave so that I could stay at the hospital with him both night and day. Remaining by his side put me in more pain, but I needed to take care of him. I wanted to be his eyes and mouthpiece.

Robert was able to come home around the same time that I finished out-processing from the Army. The church surrounded us with prayer as I cared for him in our home. I was still having pain, though, and I needed to take pain medication so that I could move enough to help him. I hated taking medication. I assume Timothy felt the same way when Paul told him to "use a little wine for your stomach's sake" (1 Tim. 5:23) to purify the water he was drinking. Timothy had to use this medicine so he could avoid stomach problems. I had to use the pain medication, so I could help my husband through his recovery. I tried to limit myself to using the medication only when I could no longer endure the pain.

Since my full-time job was now at home with my husband, I finally finished my dissertation for my doctoral degree in my spare time. I was able to defend it in late 2016. The dissertation I published for my doctorate was titled: *Exploring Coping and Adaptation in Veteran Army Nurses with Combat-Related Post-Traumatic Stress Disorder*. I had researched how nurses cope with their PTSD, the related relationship challenges PTSD created in nurses, and the struggle, and sometimes poor self-concept these nurses have. I learned that there are not enough therapeutic supports in place for nurses to teach them effective coping skills with God's blessings and mercies.

My husband healed, but he still has good and bad days. He has been able to regain enough function so that he can drive at different times. We stayed in Killeen, Texas, near Fort Hood. I felt I had moved around the world enough times. My mother is also still alive and is eighty years old at the time of this book. She remains a permanent fixture in my home. I also now care for her because she has dementia. Her ailment is and continues to be a tumultuous ride daily.

Throughout my life, God has been the Great Shepherd of it, constantly guiding me. In times when I strayed from His path, my life was difficult. I was alone, and I lost much of that inner peace. It is so easy with all the distractions of the world to deviate from His Word, but daily study and devotion to Scripture make your life easier. It is especially hard to keep your eyes on Him when you are financially struggling and must constantly work or when you are in high-stress situations. God is Omnipresent. He will always be with you. But if you turn away from Him, you won't always realize He is standing there beside you, waiting for you to turn back. It is my prayer that if you are reading this at a place in your life where you have become distracted from God's Will, that you turn back to Him and embrace Him through daily Bible reading and obeying His ten commandments.

Friends and families sometimes forsake you or persecute you for whatever reasons, but hold fast and trust God. Believe when He says, "Those who wait on the LORD shall renew their strength; they shall mount up with wings like eagles, they shall run and not be weary, they shall walk and not faint" (Isa. 40:31).

Each time I review this book I have doubts of publishing it because of the pain and hurt and sometimes categorized by God's people. But I take comfort that Jesus is my High Priest and the only one qualified to judge me. Let he that is without sin cast the first stone.

Then the mysogynistic culture in God's church sometimes leads me to ask Him if He is sure He called me. My humble prayer is that we learn to see each other through the eyes of God and come together as in the time of Pentecost!

Glossary

alto horn: a brass instrument that is sometimes called an Eb horn or tenor horn.

baptize: immersion in water that symbolizes and declares new faith in Jesus Christ.

British West Indies: a term used to describe British Empire colonies in the Caribbean that included The Bahamas (now an independent Commonwealth nation), Barbados (now an independent Common wealth nation), Bermuda (British overseas territory now), British Guiana (now the independent Commonwealth nation Guyana), Jamaica (now an independent Commonwealth nation)—which was administered together with British Honduras (now the independent Commonwealth nation Belize), Turks and Caicos (British overseas territory now) and Cayman Islands (British overseas territory now), Trinidad and Tobago (now an independent Commonwealth nation), Montserrat (British overseas territory now), Leeward Islands: Antigua and Barbuda (taken from Spain and now an independent Commonwealth nation), British Virgin Islands (British overseas territory now), St. Kitts and Nevis (now an independent Commonwealth nation), Anguilla (British overseas territory now), Windward Islands: Dominica (taken from the French and now an independent Commonwealth nation), St. Lucia (taken from the French and now an independent Commonwealth nation), St. Vincent and the Grenadines (taken from the French and now an independent Commonwealth nation), Grenada (ceded to the British and now an independent Commonwealth nation).

cardiovascular: having to do with the blood vessels and heart.

cerebella stroke: the medical condition that occurs when the blood supply is interrupted with a clot in the section of the brain that is at the back of your head on top of your spine

charge nurse: A nurse who acts like a manager for the ward in a hospital or healthcare facility. These nurses will have the same duties as other nurses, but they also have additional paperwork and supervisory duties.

church clerk: the church clerk acts as a secretary at church meetings. The clerk also keeps accurate records that include membership, committee, and church directory information.

cistern: a tank that stores water (usually rainwater) that can be used for flushing toilets and other purposes but is not safe for drinking.

clinicals: supervised learning activities where nurses practice the skills learned during nursing school in a real-world health care setting.

commissary (military): a store that sells food and supplies to military personnel.

CT (computerized tomography) scan (sometimes called a CAT or computerized axial tomography scan): a specialized X-ray that takes pictures of thin slices of your body and its tissues. These pictures are then compiled by a computer to create a three-dimensional (3-D) image of the inside of your body.

degenerative disk disease: a disease where vertebral disks become damaged over time as they thin and dry out. As the bones shift, they put pressure on the nerves and spinal cord that causes chronic pain.

dementia: a chronic mental process disorder that causes problems with memory, reasoning, and personality changes.

diabetes: a disease that occurs when your body is not breaking down sugar properly either due to not producing enough insulin or due to not being able to use the insulin produced as effectively.

dissertation: a long research paper or essay about a topic that is usually a requirement of a doctoral degree.

eAdventist.net: an online membership tracking and record keeping program for Seventh-day Adventists.

empathy: the ability to understand other people's feelings.

estrogen: a hormone naturally produced by the body that is responsible for regulating various processes related to reproduction.

false positive: a test result that shows an attribute or condition is present when it really is not.

fibroids: a non-harmful tumor made out of fibrous tissue that develops in female reproductive organs, usually on the wall of the uterus.

hormone: a chemical produced in the body that can be transported through fluids and that signals certain cells to do something.

hysterectomy: a surgical operation on a female to remove some or all of the uterus.

insulin: a hormone produced in the body that regulates the amount of glucose in the blood.

intensive care unit (ICU): a hospital ward where seriously ill patients are kept under constant watch.

incontinence: inability to control your ability to pass urine or feces.

island fever: feeling claustrophobic because of the smallness of the place where you live combined with the feeling of being cut off from the rest of the world.

leave (military): military paid vacation time that can be requested.

machete: a large knife that is considered a useful tool, and which every household in Jamaica owns. Although it can be used as a weapon, it is also used as a kitchen knife, for carving wood, to do yard work, to split coconuts, as a paddle for spanking children, and to prepare food for animals.

marijuana: a part of the cannabis plant, usually the leaf, that is smoked in cigarettes or eaten or drank for its mind-altering effects.

Medevac: medical evacuation that occurs when you transfer one patient to another hospital using a helicopter or airplane.

Medical Evaluation Board (Med Board; MEB): an informal board with at least two physicians on it that evaluates a soldier's medical background and injuries and then determines if the solder can continue serving. If the MEB finds the solder is unfit for duty, this information is then passed on to the Physical Evaluation Board (PEB) which decides if the injury was combat related, if the solder can continue in the military, and how much compensation, if any, the soldier will receive.

menopause: the point in a woman's life where she stops menstruating. This usually occurs between the ages of forty-five and fifty. In some cases, pre-menopause (the period of time prior to menopause when menstruation becomes irregular) is mistakenly called "menopause." Women who have to undergo surgery that removes certain reproductive organs will experience menopause without going through pre-menopause.

non-compliant: when a patient does not follow the recommendations of the doctor, usually by failing to take medications or attend therapy as prescribed.

nursing care plan (NCP): a document that usually contains the patient's diagnosis, his or her anticipated outcome, nursing orders, and an evaluation. The document is used to collaborate care between different nurses and for insurance purposes. It becomes a part of the patient's health record.

on-call doctor: a doctor who is ready to respond to patients usually after regular working hours. In some cases, the doctor may have a special room at a hospital where he or she can sleep and then respond whenever necessary in person. In other situations, the on-call doctor may be available only by phone for consultation.

out-processing: the necessary paperwork that ends a soldier's military tour of duty.

ovaries: a female reproductive organ.

partner: Jamaican slang term for rotating savings and credit associations. It can also refer to the draw of money one can get from these.

passport: a government issued document that certifies the identity and citizenship of the person on the document and allows that person to travel to foreign countries and return to the person's home country.

pediatric intensive care unit (PICU): a hospital ward similar to the ICU where seriously ill children are kept under constant watch.

peripheral vascular disease: disease often caused by years of smoking that causes plaques to build up on blood vessels making the passageway smaller and harder. With smaller blood vessels, less oxygen gets to the arms and legs and some of the tissue in the patient's hands and feet might die. Dead tissue can lead to gangrene and amputation.

PlayStation®: a video game console made by Sony and first released in 1994.

Post-Traumatic Stress Disorder (PTSD): a condition that occurs after witnessing physical or psychological trauma where the body continues responding to the stress even after the traumatic experience is finished. Vivid recall of the experience, disturbed sleep, and a muted response to other people and events are symptoms of the disorder.

Rastafari: Religion created in the 1930s that arose out of the Back to Africa Movement and used Hinduism superimposed on Christianity to form its basic beliefs. It is known for twisting Scripture, such as redefining the word "herbs" used in the Bible to mean the Hindu religious plant "marijuana," as a means to support its practices.

Reserve Officers' Training Corps (ROTC): a High School or college program that prepares youths to become officers in the military.

Sabbath School Superintendent: a church administrator who coordinates all the Sabbath School divisions (such as Bible Study for youth and adults, fellowship, outreach and mission) and ensures they are functioning efficiently for training Christians.

sandstorm: a windstorm in the desert that stirs up large clouds of sand.

shin splints (medial tibial stress syndrome): injury that occurs with repetitive or excess use of the muscles in the lower legs because the area is not allowed to heal properly. If untreated, it can lead to more serious conditions.

showerpipe: a pipe sticking out of the ground with water that comes out so people can stand under it to take a shower.

Sir Leonard Woolley: a British archaeologist who lived April 17, 1880—February 20, 1960. He is best known for his excavation of Ur, which is located in modern day Iraq.

station (military): military assignment to a specific place to perform a specific duty there.

switchboard: a device used for manually controlling telephone connections in a hotel or large building.

Tallil: an army base southwest of Nasiriyah. Also known as Ali Air Base and, more recently, Imam Ali Air Base.

temp job: a job position that is only contracted for a short period of time and sometimes filled by an agency that specializes in providing short term workers.

tenement yard: a multifamily multi-house living area with homes packed tightly together, sharing running water facilities and surrounded by a fence.

water truck: a truck with a large tank that carries water. The water can either be used for drinking if it is kept in sterile conditions or for other non-potable purposes such as putting out fires.

visa: an endorsement usually stamped on a passport that gives the owner of the passport the ability to enter and stay in a foreign country for a specified period of time.

ziggurat: a stepped pyramid found in the Mesopotamia region. Similar structures are found in Egypt and South America.

Bibliography

Block, Melissa, Michele Norris, and Jarret Brachman. "Expert Discusses Ties Between Hasan, Radical Imam." Episode of *All Things Considered.* NPR, November 10, 2009. https://1ref.us/1pm (accessed December 12, 2018).

Cratty, Carol. *FBI Official: Hasan Should Have Been Asked about E-Mails with Radical Cleric.* CNN, August 2, 2012. https://1ref.us/1pl (accessed December 12, 2018).

Smith, Uriah. *Daniel and the Revelation: The Response of History to the Voice of Prophecy.* Battle Creek, MI: Review and Herald Publishing Company, 1904.

Williams, Kareen Felicia. *The Evolution of Political Violence in Jamaica 1940-1980.* a dissertation: Columbia University, 2011. doi: https://doi.org/10.7916/D8WS91D7 (accessed August 2, 2021).

The Salvation Army Handbook of Doctrine, London, UK: Salvation Books, 2010.

Warren, Rick. *The Purpose-Driven Life: What on Earth Am I Here For?* Grand Rapids, MI: Zondervan, 2002.

Hill, Tiffany. "The Centenarians" *Honolulu,* October 09, 2008. https://1ref.us/1pk (accessed August 8, 2021).

Index

Abraham

Purpose Driven Life

Army

Back to Eden

Balad Air Base

British West Indies

cardiovascular unit

clinicals

Daniel and the Revelation

degenerative disk disease

discrimination

Fort Hood

Gateway computers

homelessness

hysterectomy

Imam Ali Air Base

Iraq

island fever

Jamaica Labor Party (JLP)

marriage

Martin E. Segal Company

miracle

nurse practitioner

nursing

Operation Iraqi Freedom

People's National Party (PNP)

Post-traumatic Stress Disorder (PTSD)

prayer

pregnancy

Rastafari

Rotating Savings and Credit Associations (ROSCA)

Salvation Army Church

sandstorm

shin splints

Sir Leonard Woolley

stroke

Tallil

Tripler Army Medical Center

Type II diabetes

Ur

ziggurat

TEACH Services, Inc.
P U B L I S H I N G

We invite you to view the complete
selection of titles we publish at:
www.TEACHServices.com

We encourage you to write us
with your thoughts about this,
or any other book we publish at:
info@TEACHServices.com

TEACH Services' titles may be purchased in
bulk quantities for educational, fund-raising,
business, or promotional use.
bulksales@TEACHServices.com

Finally, if you are interested in seeing
your own book in print, please contact us at:
publishing@TEACHServices.com
We are happy to review your manuscript at no charge.